C000260918

COLLINS FIELD GUIDE

BIRD CALL IDENTIFICATION

Geoff Sample

HarperCollins*Publishers*

HarperCollins*Publishers*
77–85 Fulham Palace Road
London W6 8JB

All recordings by Geoff Sample apart from the following (numbers refer to CD tracks): Roger Boughton: 36. Wryneck; 50. Brambling; 59. Bluethroat; 61 Scarlet Rosefinch. Roger Charters: 22. Turnstone; 28. Hoopoe. John Corbett: 13. Grey Plover; 28. Short-eared Owl song; 63. Snow Bunting song (2nd cut); 64. Lapland Bunting song. Simon Elliott: 16. Black-tailed Godwit; 18. Little Ringed Plover calls; 29. Long-eared Owl calls; 31. Sparrowhawk (1st cut); 32. Merlin; 62. Crossbill song. John Gordon: 65. Shore Lark song. Ivan Hills/NSA: 5. Bean Goose. Phil Hollom: 30. Little Owl; 33. Hobby. Vic Lewis/NSA: 18. Little Ringed Plover song. Richard Margoschis: 8. Lesser White-fronted Goose; 17. Avocet; 49. Waxwing; 52. Savi's Warbler; 77. Treecreeper; 86. Nightingale calls. Derek McGinn: 20. Wood Sandpiper song; 27. Long-eared Owl song; 63. Snow Bunting song (1st cut). C. & H. Myers: 2. Bewick's Swan; 6. Pink-footed Goose; 7. White-fronted Goose; 12. Spotted Redshank; 14. Wood Sandpiper calls; 15. Green Sandpiper; 21. Temminck's Stint; 25. Spotted Crake; 35. Lesser Spotted Woodpecker (2nd cut). Richard Ranft/NSA: 37. Ring-necked Parakeet. Richard Savage: 60. Red-backed Shrike. Patrick Sellar: 23. Purple Sandpiper; 58. Thrush Nightingale; 94. Snow Bunting calls; 95. Lapland Bunting calls; 97. Rock Pipit (1st cut). Lars Svensson: 96. Shore Lark calls

All recordings were made in Britain with the following exceptions: 5. Bean Goose: May, Finnish Lapland. 7. White-fronted Goose: Sept, Eire. 17. Bee-eater: May, E. France. Black-winged Stilt: June, S. France. 18. Little Tern: June, S. France. Kentish Plover: May, S. France. 22. Turnstone: June, N. Norway. 23. Purple Sandpiper: July, Spitsbergen. 25. Quail: June, S. France. 28. Short-eared Owl: June, Swedish/Norwegian Border. Hoopoe: Feb, Kenya. 36. Wryneck: Apr, Majorca. 40. Golden Oriole: May, E. France. 42. Nightingale: May, S. France. 43. Cirl Bunting: June, S. France. 44. Black Redstart: May, E. France. 45. Ortolan Bunting: June, S. France. 46. Bonelli's Warbler: June, S. France. 47. Corn Bunting: June, S. France. 48. Serin: May, E. France. 50. Brambling: June, Finland. 52. Bushcricket sp: June, S. France. 56. Cetti's Warbler: June, S. France. 58. Thrush Nightingale: May, Finland. 59. Bluethroat: June, Finland. 61. Scarlet Rosefinch: June, Finland. 63. Snow Bunting (2nd cut): June, Norway. 64. Lapland Bunting: June, Norway. 65. Shore Lark: Turkey. 69. Willow Tit (3rd cut): May, E. France. Great Tit: June, S. France. 74. Firecrest: June, S. France. 78. Kingfisher: June, C. France. 83. Black Redstart: May, E. France. Blackcap: May, S. France. 94. Snow Bunting and 95. Lapland Bunting: August, Greenland. 96. Shore Lark: June, Turkey.

First published 1998

03 02 01 00 99 98

10 9 8 7 6 5 4 3 2 1

The author hereby asserts his moral right to be identified as the author of this work and the publisher undertakes to observe such assertion and to impose the same condition on its licensees

ISBN 0 00 220122 4

Printed and bound by The Bath Press Ltd.
CD produced by DOCdata (UK) Ltd.

CD CONTENTS

Mainly non-passerines

Swan calls
1 Whooper Swan
2 Bewick's Swan, Canada Goose
3 Quick comparison of Whooper and Bewick's, Mute Swan

Grey geese calls
4 Greylag
5 Bean
6 Pinkfoot
7 Whitefront
8 Lesser Whitefront
9 Comparison low calls: Greylag, Pinkfoot, Whitefront
Comparison high calls: Greylag, Pinkfoot, Whitefront

Wader calls
10 Golden Plover, Oystercatcher, Redshank
11 Greenshank
12 Spotted Redshank, Redshank, Curlew
13 Grey Plover, Ringed Plover
14 Wood Sandpiper
15 Green Sandpiper, Common Sandpiper
16 Black-tailed Godwit
17 Avocet, Bee-eater, Black-winged Stilt
18 Little Ringed Plover, Little Tern, Little Ringed Plover (song), Kentish Plover

Wader songs
19 Ringed Plover, Golden Plover, Redshank, Greenshank
20 Wood Sandpiper, Common Sandpiper
21 Temminck's Stint, Dunlin
22 Turnstone
23 Purple Sandpiper

Crakes and rails
24 Corncrake song
25 Spotted Crake song: Quail song
26 Coot calls, Water Rail song and call, Moorhen alarm calls

Owl calls
27 Long-eared Owl song
28 Short-eared Owl song, Hoopoe song
29 Long-eared Owl female alarm and young calls, Short-eared Owl alarm calls
30 Little Owl excitement and begging calls

Small raptor calls
31 Sparrowhawk female alarm calls
32 Merlin food pass calls
33 Hobby alarm calls
34 Kestrel courtship calls

Hawk-like calls
35 Lesser Spotted Woodpecker
36 Wryneck
37 Ring-necked Parakeet, Green Woodpecker, Snipe
38 Quick comparison of raptors, Lesser Spotted Woodpecker and Wryneck

Caws and squawks
39 Carrion Crow, Rook, Jay, Magpie, Starling
40 Golden Oriole alarm call
41 Golden Pheasant song
42 Nightingale, Blackcap, Whitethroat, Sedge Warbler alarm calls

Mainly passerine songs

Dry trill songs
43 Cirl Bunting, Lesser Whitethroat
44 Black Redstart, Yellowhammer
45 Ortolan Bunting, Cirl Bunting, Dunnock trill call
46 Bonelli's Warbler, Wood Warbler

Jangling trill songs
47 Corn Bunting
48 Serin

Tinkling trills
49 Waxwing calls, Greenfinch song

Wheezing trills
50 Brambling song, Greenfinch song

Locustella warbler songs
51 Grasshopper warbler
52 Savi's Warbler, Bush Cricket spp
53 River Warbler

Acrocephalus warbler songs
54 Reed Warbler
55 Marsh Warbler, Sedge Warbler
56 Cetti's Warbler

Luscinia spp and Red-backed Shrike songs
57 Nightingale
58 Thrush Nightingale
59 Bluethroat, Winchat
60 Red-backed Shrike

Two Finch spp songs
61 Scarlet Rosefinch
62 Crossbill

Upland passerine songs
63 Snow Bunting
64 Lapland Bunting
65 Shore Lark

Pipit songs
66 Meadow Pipit
67 Tree Pipit

Mainly passerine calls

Marsh, Willow and Crested Tits
68 Marsh Tit calls, Coal tit songs
69 Willow Tit calls, Blue and Great Tit calls
70 Marsh Tit song
71 WIllow Tit song, Great Tit song, Reed Bunting call
72 Crested Tit calls, Goldcrest calls, Coal Tit calls

Crested warbler songs
73 Goldcrest
74 Firecrest

High thin 'see' calls
75 Goldcrest
76 Long-tailed Tit
77 Treecreeper
78 Robin (hard-to-locate alarm call), Dunnock, Kingfisher, Spotted Flycatcher
79 Robin 'tsee' call, Song Thrush 'tsip' call, Blackbird 'tsee' call
80 Redwing 'seeip' and 'cheg' calls
81 Fieldfare 'chack' call, Blackbird 'chuk' call, Song Thrush 'chuk' call

Sharp 'tic' and 'chak' calls
82 Hawfinch, Robin ('tic' call), Redstart
83 Black Redstart, Blackcap
84 Winchat, Wheatear, Stonechat, Wren, Great-spotted Woodpecker

'Hooeet', 'weet' and 'teu'-type calls
85 Willow Warbler, Redstart
86 Chiffchaff, Chaffinch, Nightingale, Great Tit
87 Wood Warbler, Coal Tit, Siskin

Finch contact (flight) calls
88 Brambling, Chaffinch
89 Bullfinch, Greenfinch
90 Crossbill
91 Linnet, Twite
92 Goldfinch, Siskin
93 Redpoll

More contact and alarm (flight) calls
94 Snow Bunting
95 Lapland Bunting, Yellowhammer
96 Shore Lark
97 Rock Pipit, Meadow Pipit
98 Yellow Wagtail, Grey Wagtail, Pied Wagtail, Swallow

PREFACE

Auspicious, augury, divination – all words for birdwatching when ornithologists were reckoned to be able to see more than just birds. Cast your imagination back to those days when we were held in some respect by other members of our societies; the Romans even had official state positions for us. Mind, by then superstition had crept in and things had started to go a little cranky – I wouldn't recommend waiting to start a journey until an eagle flies by on your right. (Unless you live near Falsterbo, the Bosphorus or Eilat possibly ...) On the other hand it makes a lot of sense to time planting, hunting trips and so on with the arrival of migrant species or other aspects of the bird calendar; and birds are usually the most visible indicators of subtle ecological differences between habitats, of sources of food, of intruders and so on. I always admired the Indian scouts in the old Westerns. Siberian shamans knew their birds too.

Several thousand years later and we're still at it. It must satisfy some inner atavistic longing: keeping in touch with the real world or something like that. And the first step to knowing birds is telling them apart. Using your ears gives you an amazing sense of understated power; listening in feels like a skill of ye olden days, and there's a touch of magic still in the ability to recognise species and know what birds are up to without ever having to glass them. Bird-spotter no more.

In the established tradition of British amateur natural history this work is really the product of many people, being a combination of personal observations, my own and those of friends, with the gleanings from a variety published sources – scientific and otherwise. Andrew Stuck, Pete Bull, Mark Winter, Mike Freeman, Richard Lockwood, Phil Rudkin, John Wyatt, Roy Dennis, Norman and Gail Ross and Richard Ranft have all provided a helping hand when needed, as have many others – thanks, folks. I have tried to provide references to my main sources, for those interested, but they are not comprehensive since this is intended mainly as a practical guide.

And I should offer a special thanks to all fellow wildlife recordists for their wit, hospitality and advice, and particularly those who have offered me the use of their hard-won recordings: Roger Boughton, Roger Charters, John Corbett, Simon Elliott, John Gordon, Ivan Hills, Phil Hollom, the late Vic Lewis, Derek McGinn, Richard Margoschis, Charles and Heather Myers, Richard Ranft, Phil Rudkin, Richard Savage, Pat Sellar, Lars Svenson and the British Library National Sound Archive. We all benefit from the sharing of knowledge.

Editing the material for a guide like this presents a great opportunity: a chance for me to work out much of the distinctions and interpretation for myself. So if I sound like I know it all – rest assured I'm nouveau in the knowledge. Maybe even headstrong, as fools rush in, so any errors are without doubt my own. If I have made any mistakes in my identification or if some of the recordings are of less than ideal quality, I apologise and hope this is counterbalanced by some flavour of the excitement of discovery and a feel of what it's really like to record, catalogue and investigate bird sounds.

At first sight the species included may seem a very personal or even random selection; but I hope a little thought will show some sense behind the choices. It leads on from the *Collins Field Guide Bird Songs and Calls*, with a mix of species not covered in that work and some recapping in more detail on important identification distinctions. They are almost all topics that I have been getting to grips with over the last few years myself, but I cannot claim anything definitive about it. And if I can be honest and accurate in reporting my own uncertainties as well as confidences, rather than claiming expert status in what is a difficult and often confusing area, then I hope it will be all the more useful to others trying to get to grips with the niceties of bird voices and the patterns of their utterances. Practically useful rather than pedantically comprehensive.

Species coverage is not in systematic order, though the topics begin with some correspondence to taxonomy. The aim was for a single CD of confusable calls and songs, useful for species identification and arranged for easy comparison and quick access. The focus on species identification suggested the rather general title; strictly speaking there are not just calls here, some passerine songs are included. I have used less heavy filtering or equalisation in the production process than has been usual in the past. Although this technique 'cleans up' the recorded sound, it also thins out the voices of the birds, which seems undesirable for an accurate identification guide.

Many of the cuts are shorter than intended, since I was a bit too ambitious in what could be covered in one CD. I tried to keep longer examples of the more interesting or rarer species, often with shorter examples of the commoner species for comparison. Consequently the CD feels a little crammed. The audio does not always make for easy listening; I have tried to keep in mind the idea of it as a tool likely to be dipped into here and there briefly but possibly repeatedly, rather than something that might be listened to in for long sessions. This applies to the announcements too: it began with a slightly livelier tone, which on repeated listening got irritating. Thus you have the rather dull monotone, which hopefully is less intrusive and allows you better to concentrate on the bird sounds.

Some of the species comparisons, Rock and Meadow Pipit flight calls, Winchat and Wheatear alarm calls for instance, are probably at the limits of what is practically possible for species identification in the field and then only with a 'tuned-in' ear. In describing the sounds, I have used some of the musical and impressionistic terms that science prefers to avoid ('note', 'melodic pattern', 'plaintive' etc.); from a listener's perspective I think the terms are meaningful and understood by academic and layman alike.

In the Collins Guide to Bird Songs and Calls I misidentified a Wood Warbler alarm call as a Willow Warbler call (disc1,78). I first came across the call from a bird in a family group of Willow Warblers foraging in some shrubbery and assumed it was a Willow Warbler call. Later in the day I made a closer approach to record an isolated bird giving the call, probably with head down; I usually keep my face turned away when approaching singing or calling birds as they seem to find a full frontal human face disturbing. Possibly it's just mine. Thanks to Keith Betton for pointing me in the right direction on that one.

Finally if anyone doubts the importance of sound communication in the bird world, let me draw your attention to some recent research from the Netherlands. In a study by four Dutch ornithologists into the densities of 43 species of bird breeding in woodland around roads, 26 species (60%) showed evidence of reduced density near the roads. To quote the BTO briefing: 'For roads with 10,000 cars per day the reduced density was apparent up to 1.5km from the road and for very busy roads (up to 60,000 cars per day) the effect was felt up to 2.8 kms away. The analysis clearly showed that it was the noise and not the sight of the traffic that was affecting the birds.' Species significantly affected included Buzzard, Woodcock, Cuckoo, Great and Lesser Spotted Woodpeckers, Wood Warbler, Golden Oriole and Hawfinch. Food for thought.

Geoff Sample, Northumberland, Jan. 1998

INTRODUCTION

SPECIES IDENTIFICATION

For much of the time, sound works with visuals to confirm an identification, or we may feel confident in a sound-only identification for most of the regulars in a familiar habitat, but it is not vital that we are right. Sometimes it is more important to get it right and rather difficult; for instance in atlas or other survey work, let's say amongst a flock of Linnets and other finches on your site, you once or twice hear some calls that sound different to you, Twite-like. Time is short and the light is bad; how certain can you be without a visual confirmation? It depends very much on your confidence in your own skills, since without a recording it is very difficult to corroborate a sound-only identification. Geese and swans, many of the waders, warbler alarm calls, finch, bunting and pipit flight calls are all difficult areas that need a level of familiarity before you can make confident identifications.

Visual identification of a species is facilitated by a good knowledge of plumage, which enables a precise visual description. We are hampered to a certain extent by a poor vocabulary for describing sounds and vocal attributes and we often differ in subjective impressions of the same sound. But a few obvious vocal characteristics may be overlooked which, if not decisive in themselves, may help to establish a species' identity: the rate and regularity of calling, the situation and pose of the bird, the time of day. Such aspects all contribute to the aural jizz and are more easily noted than a description of the sound.

Nevertheless it is usually a combination of musical characteristics that enables a quick vocal identification – the quality of the sound, the shape of the notes and the temporal, rhythmic and pitch patterns of repeated notes. But with calls, as opposed to song, we often have to rely more (sometimes solely) on the timbre of the sound or the tone of voice (much the same thing). The usual Golden Plover contact and alarm call (10 on the CD) is fairlydistinctive – something in the harmonic pattern of the sound – despite its simple form.

Song tends to be repeated at regular intervals or may be in long sustained passages, so identifying from calls often takes more alertness to catch a good impression from a brief snatch of sound. There are also a number of confounding factors: wind and temperature affect the transmission of sound; the density of the materials around a bird will affect its sound by colouring the sound reflections (i.e. a Robin singing from a walled corner or among the hard trunks of mature trees will sound louder and harder than one singing in the open). Distance plays tricks too, as low frequencies carry further than high frequencies; thus the song of Wood Pigeon, the winter calls of Curlew and the chiming songs of Great Tit, which sound clear and ringing at a distance, can sound surprisingly hoarse, husky or wheezy heard close-to.

The changes in timbre in some notes can also work to confuse our sense of pitch. Many bird sounds are rich in harmonics and sometimes a sound can have a fundamental falling in pitch with harmonics rising in pitch (cf Common Sandpiper alarm calls at 15).

This makes identification by sound appear ridiculously difficult, when we know that for much of the time it is not. The point I am trying to make is to warn observers to be wary of being too hasty, dogmatic and assuming with sound. I think we all have a honeymoon period when we have mastered the first phase of songs and calls, where we are optimistically over-confident with our identifications; I certainly did and still get caught out. The best identification practice is the same by eye, ear or smell: assume the most likely commoner species unless you note positive identification otherwise. Recordings work well in learning what to listen for and picking up on subtle differences, but field experience is also necessary to make confident identifications of the difficult species.

FURTHER INVESTIGATION

Some other published sources of recordings are given later in the references section. If you have time and want to look into a particular subject or several species in depth, then it is probably worth contacting the Wildlife Section of the NATIONAL SOUND ARCHIVE. They have a library of over 100,000 recordings from all around the world, which is available to the public via their listening service (free of charge, though you should arrange a visit in advance); they also have an extensive collection of literature on the subject. If you want to explore the variations in Yellowhammer song across its range, or research the calls of some of the more elusive species before a trip to some far-flung location, this is a good place to start.

WILDLIFE SECTION
The British Library National Sound Archive
96 Euston Road
London
NW1 2DB
Telephone 0171-412 7402/3

SOUND WORDS

In order to make some sense of the vocalisations we hear, we tend to provide some word of interpretation – song, songflight, contact call, 'chak' call and so on; but much of the language associated with the subject has evolved as an uneasy mix of traditional musical and behavioural terms with the more refined terminology of scientific objectivity. It is therefore probably worth reviewing this mixed language of ornithology and bioacoustics.

The intuitive distinction between song and calls works well, though is difficult to define precisely; I tend to think of song in terms of performance – as display calling that for many species (particularly the passerines) has evolved a more or less elaborate complexity. Song, advertising call, display call, and often territorial call have all been used to refer to what is much the same kind of activity, but looked at from slightly different angles. A long elaborate series of sounds is more easily thought of as song, a simpler repeated sound (cf. Spotted Crake male song, 25) as a call; when simple or 'unmusical' sounds are used by displaying birds, they have often been described as display calls, or advertising calls when there is less emphasis on posturing or movement.

For species with more complex songs, again mainly the passerines, some sing more continuously and varied, but some tend to repeat the same sequence of sounds at regular intervals; such songs are often said to be stereotyped and in many species individuals have a repertoire of several distinct song-types. Strophe has often been used to refer to each actual delivery of a song, though some observers have used 'phrase' in this sense. Species with more varied or continuous songs are often found to have a finite repertoire of phrases, combinations of which may be varied from strophe to strophe.

Softer rambling singing by both males and females is usually described as subsong; the louder song of a young male first coming into song is usually much looser than that of an adult breeder and has been called plastic song. The typical species song delivered in full voice by an adult in season is usually referred to as full song; other terms such as courtship song, communal song, flock song, describe apparent singing by birds out of the usual advertising context of song. Song-rate is used to refer to the frequency with which a bird delivers subsequent strophes of song (a high song-rate is usually particularly attractive to females).

The vocabulary of most species, as well as possibly extending to a repertoire of song-types, usually includes a number of distinct types of call (up to and over a dozen in some species). Many of these are not much use for identification since they are rarely heard by general observers, being either rarely uttered or too quiet to carry; such calls would include short-distance communication between breeding birds in a pair or several birds in a foraging flock.

As with song the names of different call-types have become a little confused by the use of various terms which are not necessarily mutually exclusive, since they are from different perspectives. To illustrate the point, the usual call given in flight by most species is a general contact and alarm call and in the case of Chaffinches is the 'tupe', 'tsup', or 'chiff' call; these are all different ways of referring to one vocalisation. The use of phonetic expressions ('tupe', 'tsk' etc.) is generally descriptive of the sound rather than defining a category of call, though BWP sometimes uses such terms to name a species' call.

'Contact call' gets used for calls which appear to have no more specialised function. Alarm calls in the non-passerines are usually loud, often harsh or shrill and frequently feature rapid repetition. For some groups including some raptors and waders, there seems to be an overlap between alarm calls and display or advertising calls (cf Turnstone and Purple Sandpiper), excited birds giving similar types of call, though the context may be different. (Some passerine species, e.g. Stonechat, when excited in alarm on breeding grounds, will sometimes break from the alarm calls into a strophe of song, often referred to as 'distraction song'.) Most passerine species have several types of alarm call and these tend to fall into two classes: thin (narrow frequency band), high-pitched, slightly down-slurred, 'see'- or 'seep'-type calls with gentle beginnings and ends, often given from more unobtrusive positions and noisier (with wide range of frequencies), more percussive and explosive, 'tchk' or 'chak' calls often rapidly repeated and given quite openly. These characteristics make the former sounds difficult for mammals and birds to locate precisely, whereas the latter are easy to locate and are the kind of call usually used to mob a predator.

For many species the same call serves for general contact and mild alarm – the 'usual call note' of traditional guides. This may show variation between different populations of a species, though on a large geographical scale rather more in the manner of a regional accent than a local dialect (which occurs in some species with song). Most calls are to an extent variable in pitch and enunciation; this allows for more accurate expression of an individual's emotional state and changes therein. There is a tendency for the voice to rise in pitch when an animal is excited or straining physically, thus flight calls are often slightly higher pitched than similar calls at rest (cf Canada Goose landing, 2).

In discussion of the constituent parts of a vocalisation, 'note' and 'syllable' tend to be interchangeable and where analysis reveals that unit to have any smaller distinct components, 'element' is used. Many calls are single notes, or monosyllabic; 'phrase' has been used to refer to call notes grouped in rhythmic patterns and for syllable groups making up a section of a song. In describing sound, 'tone' is a widely understood concept; 'timbre' refers to much the same thing, but often with an emphasis on the upper frequency harmonic content of a sound. Frequency is a measure of sound waves and is heard as pitch; low frequencies sound low-pitched – piano middle A has a fundamental of 440 cycles per second (hertz). kHz stands for kilohertz, the thousand-cycles-per-second unit.

Most real world sounds contain multiple frequencies (hence 'frequency spectrum'); the 'fundamental' frequency, which establishes the pitch of the sound, acts as a carrier for higher frequencies that give tone and timbre to the sound. In purer tones and musical sounding notes these tend to be multiples of the fundamental frequency and are called harmonics. Variations in the fundamental frequency of a sound are heard as pitch changes; regular rhythmic pitch modulation produces vibrato, but may sound more like trilling in some bird sounds.

SOUND PICTURES

There are two main ways of representing sounds in graphical form – waveform diagrams and spectrograms (also called sonograms). In order to generate these graphs a computer takes measurements through time of the electronic signal recorded from the original sound, so they present a relatively true picture of the sound as a sequence flowing from left to right. Furthermore, depending on computing power, you can zoom in to display a single phrase or note in greater resolution and pick up on the finer detail in sounds that our hearing is too coarse to discern. Thus is the ephemerality of time tamed.

Waveforms represent the loudness of a sound varying against time. The waveform (Fig.1) of a single Long-eared Owl hoot (27) shows it as a sound of less than half a second length with a fairly gentle beginning and ending (gradually tapered). The widest part shows where the sound is loudest. The time-scale on the x-axis is in milliseconds (sometimes seconds) and the y-axis is a measure of sound pressure (or electrical signal value) centred on zero. The strange lining effect is due to the rather low-resolution picture 'rounding off' finer changes in the wave.

But it does not reveal anything of the pitch or tonal quality of the sound:

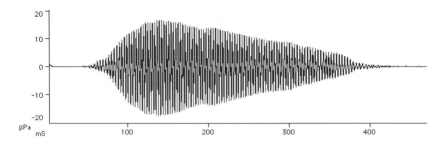

Fig. 1 Long-eared Owl – waveform of single hoot from song (27)

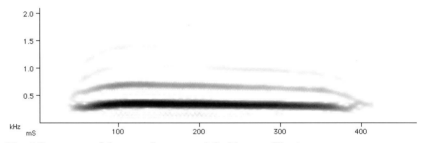

Fig. 2 Sonogram of the same Long-eared Owl hoot as Fig. 1

sonograms show the frequency content of a sound varying with time. The sonogram (Fig.2) of the same Long-eared Owl hoot shows a fundamental frequency (the lowest, boldest band) of around 300-400 Hz, rising slightly at the beginning then descending gradually in pitch; the upper parallel bands show the presence of regular harmonics colouring the sound, with the even spacing suggesting a pure or musical tone. (Note that not all male Long-eareds will necessarily show the same inflexions of pitch and timbre; it may be possible to distinguish between individuals by looking closely at the differences in these qualities of their songs, as with other species.) The x-axis is still in milliseconds, but the y-axis shows the frequency in kilohertz; the darkness represents the intensity of the frequency at that point in time.

Note the different scales on both axes in the following example (Fig.3) of the first strophe of Yellowhammer song (44), ('a little bit of bread and no chee-eese'). The waveform shows that the first part builds on repeated short sounds, followed by two sustained sounds; the sonogram also shows the rattling first part as even-pitched, but the final two notes (chee-eese) first rise

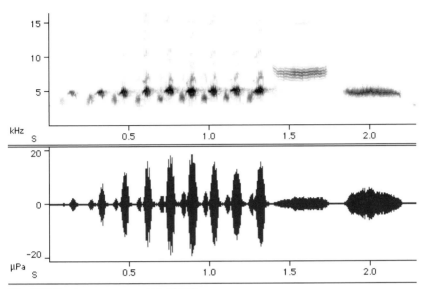

Fig. 3 Yellowhammer song (44, 0'40")

then return to the pitch of the rattle. Further, the wide frequency content of the notes suggests richly-modulated sounds. Both diagrams show that what sounds like a single repeated note to us, has two elements.

The following example (Fig.4, p. 16) shows the last strophe of Scarlet Rosefinch song (61); the waveform really gives no suggestion of what the song sounds like, but the sonogram suggests both the pure tone (clear, narrow banding) and the lilting pitch. The rising parallel bands at the end are from the Brambling-like call; the grey dusting to the right of the darker areas is from the slight reverberation of the sound in the wood.

Another technique which helps one realise the finer detail in bird sounds and song patterns, is to replay recordings at slowed-down speeds; this also lowers the pitch of the sound (halving the speed lowers the pitch an octave – half the frequency). Otherwise this is thought to approximate to how birds hear the detail in sounds with their finer temporal resolution.

For a full discussion of tone, frequency and frequency analysis with the spectrograph see 'The Tonal Quality of Bird Sounds' by P. Marler in Bird Vocalizations ed. R. A. Hinde, CUP, 1969.

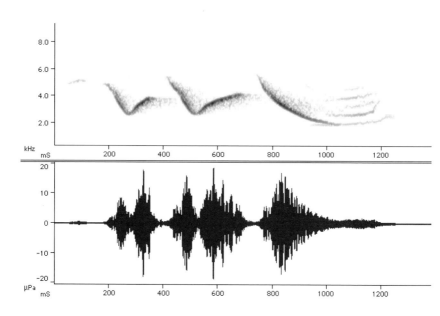

Fig. 4 Scarlet Rosefinch song (61, 0'25")

TAKING IT FURTHER

If you find the subject tempting, it is an exciting time for anyone entering the world of bird vocalisation and wildlife sound general – bioacoustics. Digital technology has simultaneously become more powerful and cheaper; Mini-disc technology has just given us a portable recorder for less than £200 with virtual CD quality and simple editing facilities. Using even a cheap micro-phone and a medium length cable it should be possible to make valuable recordings – with common sense and simple fieldcraft. Plenty of new work can be done in the garden, as there are real gaps in our knowledge and recorded coverage of even common species. Many wildlife sound recordists would admit that their ornithological knowledge is limited – myself included.

Fairly cheap sound analysis software is now available for both Mac and Windows platforms and these programs can open up a much more detailed view of sounds; most of the diagrams in this book were generated on a Mac by Canary 1.2.1 software, available from Cornell Laboratory of Ornithology. One of the great benefits of working with sound on the computer is that you have almost instant access to any part of any recording on your hard-disc. You can listen to the opening phrase of a Snow Bunting song, then at a click of the mouse – less than a second – you can be hearing the opening phrase of another Snow Bunting song or any other recording available to the program.

You may be interested in joining the WILDLIFE SOUND RECORDING SOCIETY. The society is based in Britain and the majority of members are amateur wildlife sound recordists; it is not a practice for which there is an established route to a professional career nor many jobs, so 'amateur' work, as in certain other areas of zoology, is very important. A journal is published twice a year with articles ranging from site reports, studies of individual species to reviews of recording equipment and techniques. An audio programme of members' recordings is produced 4 times a year and copies (cassette, open reel, DAT & mini-disc) circulate to members only. Local meetings, week-ends at field centres and longer expeditions are organised by and for members. The Curator of the Wildlife Section of the National Sound Archive can put you in touch with the membership secretary. Naturally birds, the most vocal group of animals, provide much of the subject matter, but orthopterans (grasshoppers and crickets), amphibians, particularly frogs and toads, and many groups of mammals including cetaceans and bats all add to the variety of the acoustic landscape.

And if my recordings help draw you further into that landscape, then I have done my job; we have such a brief span in which to realise and enjoy its subtle and rich flavours.

SPECIES ACCOUNTS

Swan calls   1

Whooper Swan, Bewick's Swan, Canada Goose, Mute Swan

Distinguishing between the calls of different swan and geese species takes some practice; since all the calls are rather variable in their voicing, between different individuals and different situations, it is a case of recognising a few typical motifs and getting a feel for general differences of voice. The first example of **Whooper Swan** features calls from a small flock of around 20 birds flying north over a wooded valley at no great height early in the morning. After the first loud whoop several birds give a series of even, short hoo's at the same pitch; this has been referred to as the flight call (BWP) and likened to a motor-horn (TYBS) - note the slight reediness. The other calls, fairly typical from an excited flock (classic whooping calls) are often up-slurred in pitch, with a moaning quality (compared to Bewick's yelp) in a voice, typically louder, deeper and more trumpet-like (Macmillan); note how the pitch keeps varying from call to call.

The example of **Bewick's Swan** is of a small flock on water coming up to roosting time. At the beginning the calling is relaxed, with sustained crooning calls typical of birds on water; towards the end the birds become more excited and the calls include castanet-like clattering, reminiscent of cranes (TYBS). The whoops in contrast to those of Whoopers are thinner-voiced yelps, sometimes with a creaky, squealing quality when the calls become more excited; the first loud yelp in the example (repeated at intervals) is distinctive with a quick rise and fall in pitch. The 'soft, pleasing, rather hollow *oop oop*' referred to as characteristic in the Macmillan Guide is in a similar voice to the sustained calls at the start of the example, but rather Hoopoe-like in form (cf. the first example in JCR). Both species give similar long, sustained, hoots in a rich falsetto, referred to as Triumph calls (BWP).

In general Whooper's calls have a slightly reedy bugling quality often referred to in guides; **Canada Goose** calls are really quite similar to the louder flock calls of Whooper but with an even more emphatic reedy timbre. Note how the pitch of the calls falls once the bird has come to rest on the water.

The first cut of **Whooper Swan** is from the start of the example earlier; the other three cuts are calls of single birds in low flight, near landing or taking off: the second and fourth from one bird of a pair and the third from one of

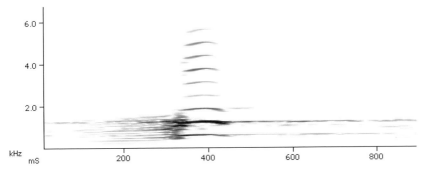

Fig. 5 Canada Goose call (2, 0'45"). The burst of upper harmonics gives the bugle effect.

a small group over mudflats. The Bewick Swan cuts are from the previous example.

The first example of **Mute Swan** features typical threat snorts at me from two birds at dusk; there were around 150 swans scattered on this coastal pool in June - presumably non-breeders and failed breeders. In the second example I had accidentally disturbed a group of 6 immatures roosting on a small lake in the pre-dawn darkness; these were some of the calls. The species also has some display calls associated with breeding, but these are not particularly loud either.

Grey geese calls 4

Greylag, Bean, Pinkfoot, Whitefront, Lesser Whitefront

In all these species calls tend to have two extremes of voicing: lower pitched honks in a full voice and higher-pitched squeals or yelps in a thinner, almost falsetto voice; calling patterns frequently feature series of each separately and mixed, often with confusing in-between variations. Excited varied calling, especially from larger groups of birds, has a gabbling sound often referred to, especially appropriate to Greylag and Bean. Experienced listeners also tune in to this over-all flock sound. The following order is in perceived similarity of voice (general timbre and pitch).

The first example of **Greylag Goose** features the contact-alarm calls of a single bird in flight when there was a stream of scattered individuals and small groups moving around adjacent coastal flats in winter; note the gruff, hoarse quality to the loud single honks. The second two examples feature more excited calls from pairs of birds in spring in potential breeding sites, with other birds nearby in the first case and just a flying pair in the second; the patterns of calling and the repeated motifs in the second (notice the typical 3 and 4 honk runs) are similar to calls from birds in excited flocks (cf. in the distance in the first example).

The voice of **Bean Goose** has a hard nasal resonance in contrast with Greylag's hoarse, more guttural sound; excited calling has more of a cackling quality compared to Greylag's gabble. Calls are also thought to be generally lower-pitched (TYBS), but the relative difference is not something easily picked up in the field, listening to a single species. The calls in the example are most comparable with the second Greylag example; the recording is of two Beans risen from a forest marsh, calling in flight; note they are probably of the taiga species (*fabalis*).

In comparison with the previous two species **Pink-footed Goose** has a slightly higher-pitched, thinner-sounding voice, still with a burr, but less rough. The calls in the example are from scattered birds leaving their overnight roost. The rather formal 'ang-anks' (Macmillan) at the beginning still have something of the reedy, full honks of Greylag in comparison with the thinner, slurred doubles of White-front following. The more animated calls of several birds towards the end have an over-all cackling sound with a squeakiness in both high and low calls, not apparent in the two species earlier.

The calls of **White-fronted Goose** are characterised by heavier pitch-modulation, often with up- and down-slurs in the same syllable and a rather gentler, more 'musical' timbre to the voice. In comparison with the 'aa' and 'ee' sounds of Pinkfoot, Whitefronts generally have a more 'ow' sound - calls often being rendered something like 'kow-lyow' (BWP). More excited calling from a larger group of birds gives an impression of slightly hysterical, zany yelping. The example features birds, probably of the Greenland population, flying in from an overnight roost offshore.

The calls of **Lesser White-fronted Goose** are similar to those of White-front, but with quicker phrasing and in a slightly higher-pitched, shriller voice; typical flight call is well rendered 'dyee-yik' (LJ). I do not feel that an identification of this species by voice alone could be reliable without much experience.

The brief cuts are in the order Greylag, Pinkfoot and Whitefront low-voiced calls, then Greylag, Pinkfoot and Whitefront high-voiced calls.

Wader calls & songs 10

Golden Plover, Oystercatcher, Redshank, Greenshank, Spotted Redshank, Curlew, Grey Plover, Ringed Plover, Wood Sandpiper, Green Sandpiper, Common Sandpiper, Black-tailed Godwit, Avocet, Bee-eater, Black-winged Stilt, Little Ringed Plover, Little Tern, Kentish Plover, Temminck's Stint, Dunlin, Turnstone, Purple Sandpiper

With wader calls sometimes the phrasing or pattern of calling may be distinctive, but, especially with monosyllabic calls, identification is usually based on recognising timbre and to a certain extent pitch. Wader songs tend to be marked by rolling repetition – a faster trill, a more deliberate repetition of a single note or the continuous repetition of a simple motif.

Golden Plover contact calls are haunting in their simplicity. This example is from the breeding grounds in Spring; calling in winter flocks becomes more modulated and varied, and seems to take place as a kind of communal song. With very little modulation, the even harmonics give the distinctive, pure tone.

Oystercatcher general contact calls may be a monosyllabic 'peep' or with a more or less emphatic introductory syllable as in 'tupeep' - both forms uttered in the example on CD; the crescendo trill building into repetitions of the call is diagnostic of the species. Compare the voice with the simpler variations of Grey Plover calls (13).

Redshank and **Greenshank** contact and alarm calls are frequently similar in both form and tone. Both species give flutey-voiced 'teu', 'tyoo' or 'tchew' calls for general contact and alarm; the voice becomes shrill with rapid repetition of a sharper call when a bird is excited or alarmed. The differences in voice are

Fig. 6 Golden Plover call (10, 0'16"). Note the slight rise in pitch and precise harmonics.

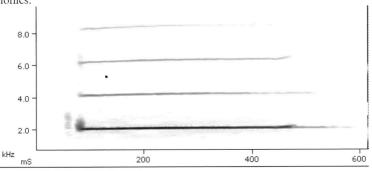

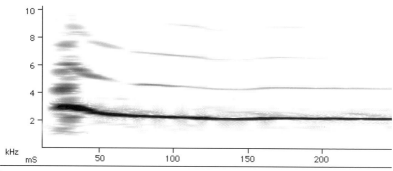

Fig. 7 Redshank call (10, 0'52").

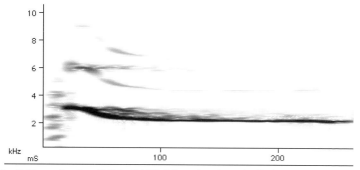

Fig. 8 Greenshank call (11, 0'10"). Note the close similarity to Redshank.

slight, but with experience can be appreciated; certain calling patterns are fairly diagnostic. The 'teuhuhu' pattern is diagnostic of Redshank, whereas Greenshank frequently gives triple repetitions of the full 'tyoo' call.

The most frequently heard call of **Spotted Redshank** is the general contact and alarm call. Disyllabic, less pure and whistling than the usual calls of Redshank and Greenshank; approaching Curlew or even the Godwits in tone. But a much briefer call than any of Curlew's calls. **Redshank** occasionally give slightly wheezy or huskier sounding calls, of variable form and sometimes broken into several syllables; these have occasionally fooled me into thinking there was a more unusual species about. Several examples are given for comparison. In winter **Curlews** seem to lose the clear piping tone (except possibly for the occasional trills) and the usual contact and alarm calls have a distinctly hoarse timbre if heard clearly; or this may be an effect of different acoustic conditions.

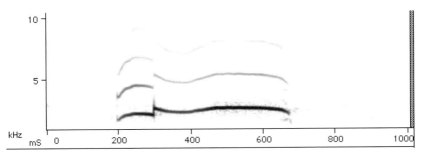

Fig. 9 Grey Plover call (13, 0'22"). Note the break in the continuity of pitch, which gives the yodel effect.

Grey Plover calls are typically a clear 'wee-oo-ee', (Macmillan) ('pleeoo-wee' LJ); but variations are frequently simpler in form, as many of the calls here. These may be the calls of young, immature birds or could represent the intrinsic variability of the call. The tone of the voice may be reminiscent of Curlew in the breeding season, but calls are shriller and thinner-sounding (corresponding to the smaller size of the bird), and are usually loudly voiced and carry well. The usual calls of **Ringed Plover** , the general contact and alarm calls, 'kayu', 'tooip' (LJ), 'queep' (HFP), 'poo-ip' (Macmillan), are more variable than the guides tend to imply and may approach those of Grey Plover in tone and form, but are not voiced anything near as loudly, are softer-toned, more abrupt and generally disyllabic with the second rising. Three examples are given: in the first several birds are calling, prior to much display (with a Dunlin contact call audible in the distance); in the second, the bird is calling in alarm near a breeding site; in the third, recorded by a gravelly moorland pool visited by Ringed Plover, I didn't see the bird - you may disagree with my identification. Compare these calls with the much shriller, trilled calls of Little Ringed Plover later.

These **Wood Sandpiper** calls tend to be the most commonly-heard outside the breeding season, particularly in flight, and are the most distinctive. More alarmed birds, particularly on breeding grounds, give a more shank-like, but sharper, repeated 'chip', which may be interspersed with a softer repeated 'weep' call. Note the two calling patterns - a longer, even sequence descending slightly in pitch and doubles that rise slightly in pitch. With apologies to Charlie Myers, who was reluctant for me to use this recording because of the train in the background; nevertheless the calls are clear, showing the slightly slurred, squeaky timbre and recorded in Britain.

The equivalent contact-alarm call of **Green Sandpiper** is typically given in a rhythmic motif with a lower note introducing a series of 3 or 4 higher notes, giving a slightly hysterical giggling impression and they are excitable birds. The individual notes are less clipped than Wood and heavily up-slurred, though if a bird becomes agitated, its calls approximate to a high-pitched, chipping alarm call. The several birds calling in the example show the range of variation. The equivalent call of **Common Sandpiper** is very similar to that of Wood Sandpiper but in a thinner voice with less clipped and slurred notes; shorter (2 or 3 notes often) variations on this call are often heard in spring, but in the same distinctive, high-pitched, clear whistling voice. The second example is the drawn-out 'ssiep' alert call of BWP, frequently heard from birds disturbed near their nest.

Both Black-tailed and Bar-tailed Godwits have a slight wheeziness to their voices reminiscent of Lapwing. The recording begins with excited 'wicka'-type calls from a number of **Black-tailed Godwits** in a flock in the mid-distance; then a single bird passes singing and later a single bird passes calling. With this species, singing and calling are not easily separated.

With **Avocet**, it is mainly a case of recognising the voice; with experience the simple repetitive calling patterns may become more familiar. The calls in the recording are from an adult to young after some Black-headed Gulls had passed too close. The basic call is varied in loudness, shrillness and timbre slightly according to mood.

Bee-eater general alarm and contact calls ('quip') are very similar sounding - something to keep in mind if looking for Bee-eaters and certainly the species occur together at a number of sites in mainland Europe (Camargue).

Black-winged Stilts have quite a varied repertoire of call types, most uttered with a fairly distinctive sharp creakiness to the voice. The calls in the example here are from a pair settling down after the return of one to the nest.

In the example of **Little Ringed Plover**, this female sounds a little nervous, but the calls seem basically the general contact and alarm call, a disyllabic 'peeu' (1 in BWP). Heard close-up the call is shrill rather than ringing and a trilling creakiness is detectable. But the sonogram reveals further differences in these calls and they may include the alarm threat call (2 in BWP), sounding more speeded-up and clipped.

Little Tern calls are broadly similar, but have a yelping quality from the slurring of the pitch.

The second example of **Little Ringed Plover** features a bird in display-flight singing a typical rhythmically-repeated, creaky, trilled motif, quite tern-like in feel. Song is also given from the ground (BWP).

This example of **Kentish Plover** is of several birds, possibly non-breeders, at the waters edge in late spring; the calls here seem to include 1 and 4 from BWP.

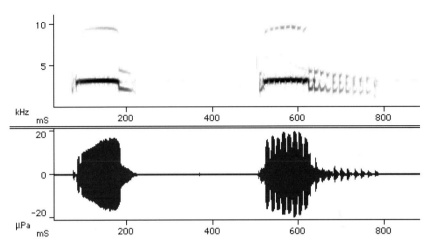

Fig. 10 Little Ringed Plover calls (18, 0'03"). These are the first two calls – note the different voicings.

To introduce the songs and display calls of some of the rarer breeders for Britain, we recap on the songs of the following: **Ringed Plover** - an accelerating repetition of a wheezy 't'weeu'-type motif (two birds singing at once here), **Golden Plover** - a brief repetition of a flutey 'yipiyoo'-type motif ('churilee' in TYBS), **Redshank** - a repeated, flutey 'tuleeoo'-type motif (introduced by the copulation rattle), **Greenshank** - a sometimes very lengthy repetition of a clangorous 'klu-hi'-type motif; the exact motif differs slightly between individuals. The calls at 11 also end with song.

Wood Sandpiper song is closest to that of Greenshank - a repetition of a slightly clangy 'kleehu' motif; but the repetitions are faster, in short bursts (always?) and the voice is higher-pitched, thinner and with more of a whistling timbre.

The **Common Sandpiper** song in the example begins with a continuous, but pulsating trilling, which then becomes a repeated motif of 5-note runs rising slightly in pitch. Song is apparently given by both sexes and is often uttered in flight as here. The notes of the trills have a sibilance very similar to those of **Temminck's Stint** and the rate of the trill is about the same, when excited at the beginning; but note the more sustained, even passages in the latter. Nevertheless in a passage of singing (there are consecutive recordings

25

in the example), the trill is varied slightly and may seem to rise and fall (BWP). Song is delivered in a hovering display flight. Outside the breeding season Little Stint is thought to be the more vocal of the two species.

Another small wader with a fast trilling song is **Dunlin**, but the notes of the trill are harder, slightly shrill and without the sibilance of the previous two species; again song is usually delivered in flight and the overall crescendo pattern in the example is typical. If you listen closely the song is actually a series of shorter trills all run together. Note the repeated croaking or humming call which is commonly heard on the breeding grounds with song. The generally-used call is a short, quite hard trill, 'treer', in a similar voice to song.

The **Turnstone** calls in the example have a similar hard shrillness to Little Ringed Plover calls (cf. 18) and are the chattering alarm calls reported in BWP as given strictly in the breeding season when they may function as a form of singing. This lead me to think they might be display calls, but compare the example of songs given in JCR which are extended (2-3 seconds), chattering trills on a single, hard, sometimes squeaky note, with a slight crescendo.

Likewise song or display calls of **Purple Sandpiper** seem hard to define; according to BWP it is variable in length and complexity and appears to be more an amalgam of vocabulary. The short trills in the example seem to be the announcement call, one of the components of song, and the other calls sound like the general contact 'keutt' (LJ). In full song from displaying birds, the announcement trills become more extended and repeated with variations and other Dunlin-like, rising 'sweer' calls may be included (cf. JCR).

Crakes and rails   24

Corncrake, Spotted Crake, Quail, Water Rail, Coot, Moorhen

The songs of Corncrake and Quail were covered in Bird Songs and Calls, but since these species are rarely glimpsed in their usual habitats and the male's song almost always provides the only indication of the species' presence, brief examples are included here for quick reference. Spotted Crake song, when heard, is really quite unmistakable; but it is now such a rare bird in Britain, that it may be tempting for an enthusiastic ear at a distance to mistake one of the other species for it. These last species, Coot, Water Rail and Moorhen all produce a wide range of sounds, some unusual and strange.

Corncrake song is unmistakable really. Peak of male vocal activity is in darkness between 11 pm and 3 am BST, though a few individuals may sing intermittently during the day. Birds also may sing on migration.

Likewise **Spotted Crake** male song is unmistakable when heard clearly;

but I have found myself wondering optimistically about a few distant sounds that I am sure in retrospect were from the more common species. Even at a distance the monotonously regular repetition of a single note should be apparent except in a high wind; then note the penetrating, 'whiplash' tonal element. In the example, the rate is quite slow, but still very even; birds may deliver their songs at a much faster rate and make momentary pauses (cf. example in JCR where 2 males are singing within earshot). The three-note song of **Quail** is probably closest in tone, but is hardly mistakable; on the other hand Coot, Water Rail and Moorhen all frequently give single note calls regularly repeated and are likely to occur alongside Spotted Crake.

The first example of **Coot** is territorial 'kowping', clearly tonally different, with quicker repetition and not sustained for long periods like the crakes; likewise in the second example with the 'pit' contact calls which are also less penetrating (there are more popping 'phut'-type and high-pitched 'zit'-type variants to this call). The first example given of **Water Rail** is the courtship song, the trill at the end indicating a female (cf. BWP). It is often sustained for long periods through the night, but in something like this crescendo motif; the second example I suspect is of a general contact and alarm call and may be given louder with an explosive, penetrating quality (cf. 'advertising song of male' in NSA), but has a percussive rather than whiplash tone and is not usually sustained for long periods. Although the examples of **Moorhen** calls given here would not be easily confused with Spotted Crake song, there is a similarity of tone and calls of this type are variable, can be quite explosive and carry well and can be repeated monotonously for long periods.

The song of Little Crake is broadly similar to Spotted Crake with repetitions of a single higher-pitched, croakier note, though calling patterns may approach those of Water Rail, as series of repetitions accelerate and fade. The song of Baillon's Crake is a repeated short mechanical trill of around 8 to 10 notes, suggesting a large grasshopper; heard at any distance it sounds more like a croak. Burton and Johnson point out it may be confused with Common Frog *Rana temporaria*, Edible Frog *R. esculenta* and European Tree Frog *Hyla arborea* or Stripeless Tree Frog *H. meridionalis* (and Little Crake with the tree frogs).

Owl calls 27

Long-eared Owl, Short-eared Owl, Little Owl, Hoopoe

Generally regarded as the most nocturnal of our owls, **Long-eared Owl** is an elusive species and often noted as probably under-recorded in survey work. The male's song, heard in late winter and early spring (at roosts as well as breeding sites?), is a fairly unmistakable 'whoo', but really quite similar to Eagle Owl song, though much less loud and deep; and though it may carry quite well in calm and quiet conditions, it is probably easily 'overlooked' at any distance where sheep are present and vocal. Females have a similar song, but in a hoarser, cracked voice (LJ says clearer and more drawn-out, but cf. example in JCR); remember that young Tawny Owls give a wide range of unusual hoots and calls, and excited adult males repeat single hoots, but drawn-out and tremulous. Note the low pitch of Long-eared and the regular repetition. (There is further discussion and a sonogram of Long-eared Owl song in Sound Pictures on p. 12).

Short-eared Owl song is unlikely to be confused with Long-eared, but is an easily overlooked sound, especially at the distance it is likely to be heard; it consists of short bursts of staccato hoots, here sixteen to seventeen in around 4 seconds, repeated at intervals (often longer than in the example here). I have mistaken it with Lapwing wing-beats, Stock Dove song and on the first hearing at a long distance wondered about Hoopoe. An example of **Hoopoe** song follows for comparison - much thinner-sounding and higher-pitched (closer to Tengmalm's Owl – LJ) and typically in 2-3 note sequences at short intervals.

Good evidence of successful breeding by **Long-eared Owl** is provided in the early summer by the squeaking hunger calls of the fledgling young and the alarm and contact calls of the adults: the thin bark in the example (from a female on the wing) is typically given as a double and there are even thinner, squealing contact calls. Compare these with the barking alarm calls of **Short-eared Owl** where a hunting bird flushes some Red Grouse. I had hoped for a recording at something less than the three to four hundred metres of this one, but could not locate one in time; I have included this as better than nothing. The calls are not so shrill or explosive as Long-eared and in display may be more drawn-out with a distinct crescendo. Both Short-eared and Long-eared indulge in wing-clapping displays.

Little Owl calls have been referred to as 'a shrill rather plaintive "kiu"' (PMH), 'a loud, ringing "kiew, kiew"' (HFP), but there are other frequent calls. Alarm and contact calls are generally more explosive, clipped 'kew'-type notes, often rapidly repeated (and hawk-like); the more drawn, mewing 'weeoo'-type sounds in the example of a male bringing food back to its mate on the nest, are the 'excitement' calls of BWP. The shrill tone is also evident in the more formal 'hoop' of the male song (cf. Bird Songs & Calls).

Small raptor calls

Sparrowhawk, Merlin, Hobby, Kestrel

Many of the larger as well as the smaller raptors, including Peregrine Falcon and Goshawk, give calls of two kinds: 'yikkering' or 'kekking' and squealing or 'eeping'. Many raptors can be very vocal at times, particularly in courtship, when alarmed near the nest and when in family parties with fledged young in summer. But generally for much of the time birds of all species are silent, especially away from the vicinity of the nest area. For most general birders I suspect that like me only on rare occasions will calls be useful in identifying raptors to species level, but probably most useful is a little knowledge of small raptor calls: the larger raptors tend to be more obvious to the eyes. Beware that the squealing calls of raptors, especially the hunger calls of the young of larger raptors (including Buzzard, Goshawk, Honey Buzzard) can sound very similar to various gull species calls (including Common Gull, Herring Gull).

For a quick comparison of individual calls of these raptors and the most similar of the hawk-like species go straight to (37).

Sparrowhawk yikkering type calls are given in alarm and also by the male when returning to the female with food, when they can be quite unobtrusive even at a hundred metres in woodland. The rate, at about 7 'kek's per second, is similar to Merlin but faster than either Kestrel or Hobby.

Simon Elliott's recording of the **Merlins** is actually of the food pass, with the fast chattering call from the male and 'eeping' calls from the female. This is usually the way with other raptor species when the male brings food; but Simon has a recording of a male Sparrowhawk with food on its plucking post giving a squealing call for its mate.

In the example given of **Hobby** alarm calls, the notes are repeated more slowly, emphatically and with a fuller voice; it is easier to hear the 'kyew'-like slurred pitch of the note (cf. Wryneck following). In the example given in NSA, the bird perched in the foreground, the male, is calling with faster repetition and could more easily be confused with Kestrel. Hobbies also give 'eeping' calls, in a similar voice to Kestrel but usually at a much faster rate (around 2-3 per second).

In the first example the **Kestrel** call is composed of sharper, more percussive, single 'ki'-type repeated notes, whereas the Hobby's notes are more drawn-out; the Hobby call could even be considered fast 'eeping'. The second Kestrel example features the 'eeping'-type calls of this species - described as 'querulous calls of a female' in NSA; I suspect that these calls also were from the female, but could not see the birds during recording. The third example features short clicking calls, which I suspect were given just before or during mating. Richard Margoschis has recorded Peregrine Falcon giving similar types of calls at the nest during copulation (featured on WSRS circulating tape 105).

Hawk-like calls 35

Lesser Spotted Woodpecker, Wryneck, Ring-necked Parakeet, Green Woodpecker, Snipe

A number of species are frequently cited as sounding similar to the previous raptors. The notes of the **Lesser Spotted Woodpecker** call are tonally similar to the Kestrel and delivered at around the same speeds, but higher-pitched and shriller (appropriate to a sparrow-sized bird). This call, most frequently heard in the spring, may serve as song in addition to drumming. Birds also call with single 'kik' notes. The call in the second example has a richer, less shrill tone.

Wryneck song is probably closer in sound to the Hobby calls in both the rate of repetition and the drawn-out 'kew' tone of the individual notes; and Hobbies may call in longer bursts than the example earlier.

Ring-necked Parakeets have now become quite numerous in a number of areas in Britain and mainland Europe; flight calls are generally a Hobby-like 'kew-kew-kew' repetition as in this example, which includes more varied calls from a group of four birds about to leave for their roosting site. Note the bubbling wheeziness in the voice (a hint of Budgie?).

Neither **Green Woodpecker** nor **Snipe** should really be confused on sound with any of previous raptors, but there is something hawk-like in the form of the first and the tone of the second species and Goshawk 'kekking'-type calls can sound very similar to Green Woodpecker (cf. TYBS Coniferous/Mixed Woods).

The first example of Green Woodpecker song is typical in form with a slight decrescendo to a definite ending, the second is more uneven, but note a ringing, almost wader-like (Oystercatcher?) tone to the end of the elements. Snipe song, heard only in the breeding season I think, is a sort of slow 'yikker', 'chipper' (NSA) or 'tick-a' (LJ) - take your pick; the example sounds monosyllabic, but frequently it is a more audible disyllabic repetition and given in flight as well as perched.

Quick comparison of small raptors and similar calls 38

Sparrowhawk, Merlin, Kestrel, Lesser Spotted Woodpecker, Hobby, Wryneck

Caws & squawks 39

Carrion Crow, Rook, Jay, Magpie, Starling, Golden Oriole, Golden Pheasant, Nightingale, Blackcap, Whitethroat, Sedge Warbler

Distinguishing between Carrion Crow and Rook by tone of voice is a fine point for the tuned-in ear. **Carrion Crow** advertising calls are typically an even series of 3 to 5 very similar caws repeated at intervals; this could be called song, but with the corvids many people refer to the softer, guttural, warbling vocalisations as song or subsong. Roger Charters also sent me a rare recording of a loud Jay song, a clear, ringing 'wee-yoo'. The **Rook** calls given are from a bird in flight; apart from differences in the tone of voice, Rook calls are much more varied, and are less prone to repetitions of stereotyped patterns - at least in the case of crow-like 'caws'.

Note the basic similarity between the voices of **Jay** and **Magpie**, though the chattering or rattling patterns to Magpie calls usually provide a clear distinction. I have some recordings of squealing 'caws' from the Wyre Forest (where these two examples are from) which are either Jay or Magpie, but I cannot decide. These **Starling** alarm calls, from a bird near the nest, have something of the same sound quality, but are not such far-carrying, explosive vocalisations. Heard at a distance the high frequencies that give the churring edge will be less noticeable and the tone will approach that of these **Golden**

Fig. 11 Starling call (39, 0'54"). Note the wide frequency content, giving the harsh, noisy tone.

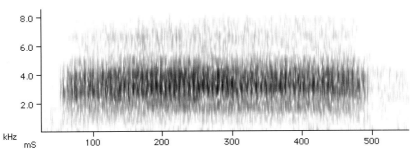

Oriole calls. Golden Orioles give other calls with a similar, sometimes even more Starling-like tone of voice, when alarmed (cf. JCR).

Golden Pheasant male song is something of a squawking shriek, here repeated but often given singly. This bird was singing from halfway up a small tree in a dense Yew wood. The soft, sweet clucking note near the start is also from the same bird, and seems to be part of the song, though only audible at close range. Lady Amhurst males have a trisyllabic display call 'huc,ca-huc' in a voice somewhere between Pheasant and Golden Pheasant, also accompanied by softer flutey 'cluck's.

These next calls were recorded without seeing the bird; there had been a **Nightingale** in this spot around five minutes earlier giving the 'weet' call (cf. 85), which I wanted to record, but there was also a male Blackcap about. I was lucky to record a Nightingale making a similar sound between song bursts, or as part of its song, a week later in the same region, which suggests that these are Nightingale calls, with a buzzy tone unlike the croaking alarm calls frequently published. (cf. BWP)

These **Blackcap** alarm calls, recorded fairly close to a bird calling in a hedge, would not be audible at any distance and are not heard as often as the sharper alarm 'tchk's. But they make for a good comparison with the common and sometimes variable calls of Whitethroat. Note that it sounds like the bird breaks into several high-pitched alarm calls of the hard-to-locate type, towards the end, where the Magpie's 'chak's in the background become more squealing. **Whitethroats** readily give these alarm calls; two examples are given here, the second lower pitched. The calling rate here is fairly typical but may speed up if a bird is agitated; note that Whitethroats, like so many of the warblers, use a variety of alarm calls, including a more Blackcap-like or Reed Warbler-like 'tsuk' and some Blue Tit-like motifs.

Continuing the theme, **Sedge Warbler** alarm calls, often also described as 'churring' have a more rasping or rattling sound quality; it takes a little practice to distinguish the similar, but lower-pitched and more grating call of Reed Warbler from this one. Garden Warbler also has a churring alarm call.

Other notable squawks include the deep, gruff calls of many species of heron, of which the 'frank' call of the Grey Heron is a typical example.

Dry trills   43

Cirl Bunting, Lesser Whitethroat, Black Redstart, Yellowhammer, Ortolan Bunting, Bonelli's Warbler, Wood Warbler

A number of passerine species have similar sounding songs that are little more than trills in form; and where some of the species occur together, it can be easy to misidentify songs. The buntings tend to stereotyped songs, repeating the same song (type) a number of times almost identically, then switching to another type and repeating that for a while; and in many bunting species the notes have a slightly hard timbre, reminiscent of insect stridulation, that gives the song the feel of a dry trill. The trills of Bonelli's and Wood Warblers are more liquid-sounding in contrast, the notes being less percussive, and more sibilant rather than grating.

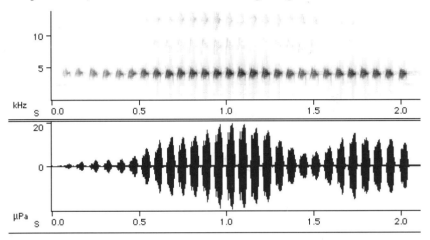

Fig. 12 Cirl Bunting song (43, 0'13")

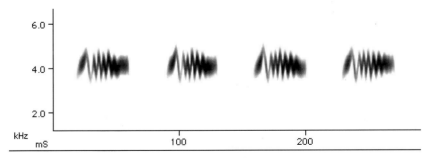

Fig. 13 Detail: the main frequency component of four notes of the song in higher resolution.

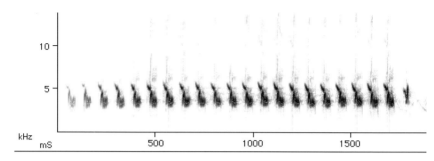

Fig. 14 Cirl Bunting song (43, 0'31").

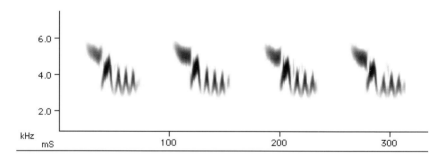

Fig. 15 Four notes in higher resolution.

Cirl Bunting songs are typically even-pitched trills of around 1.5 to 2 seconds, with rattling, discrete repetitions of a single note. The higher resolution sonograms show that what sounds like a single note may be more complex in structure. The rate is quite fast - about 14 elements per second in the first song; the variations in intensity or loudness are due to a variable breeze affecting the sound transmission and possibly the bird turning its head, rather than anything intrinsic to the song. Other song-types feature more Yellowhammer-like notes, more sibilant notes (cf. NSA, second example, but this still has something of the sharp attack, with the note suggesting Tree Pipit); and slightly faster versions with a sharper rattling sound like 'trrrrr'.

The trilled or rattling part of **Lesser Whitethroat** song is superficially rather similar in form to Cirl Bunting, though in shorter phrases - typically a second or less in length and at a slightly slower speed. But the timbre is less

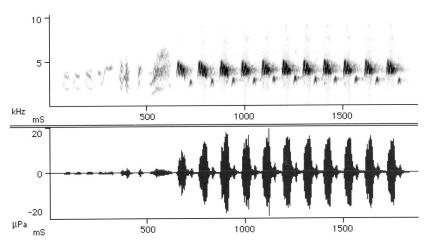

Fig. 16 Lesser Whitethroat song (43, 0'50").

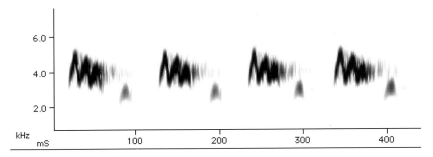

Fig. 17 Four notes in higher resolution.

percussive and more Chaffinch-like and the notes are revealed in the sonogram to have two more separate elements.

At a distance **Black Redstart** male song gives the impression of a short, bunting-like trill; but note the slower speed, with only around 4 or 5 notes, and rather shrill, squeaky timbre, though the latter is variable and can have a more liquid tone (cf. example from London in NSA). Heard from a little closer, the strange, scratchy phrases become evident, very similar to certain phrases in Wheatear songs; BWP quotes a fine description from Dare (1953) 'spluttering or crackling like wireless atmospherics'. The species song is also revealed to have a more elaborate structure: a slightly warbled trill, followed by a pause, then the scratchy phrasing introducing a louder trill. In our example the second song misses the introductory phrase. The **Yellowhammer** songs in the example feature a trill superficially similar to the previous species' songs; the trill is at the relaxed pace of Black Redstart, but the notes have a distinctly bunting timbre, more akin to Cirl, though the repetition is shorter in length, tends to build to a crescendo and often rises in pitch (as in the example). Note the missing ending on the second song. A sonogram of the first song is featured and discussed in Sound Pictures on p. 15).

Ortolan Bunting songs take the theme further with a slower, lazier repetition of a richer, note with more elision, giving the impression of a minimalist. Song-types vary, but southern types are usually no more than a 2 or 3 note repetition with an ending note, often featuring slurred pitch; JCR gives two examples of Scandinavian birds, whose songs are rather different - several repetitions of one note lead in several repetitions of a lower note. **Dunnock** have a rather insect-like alarm call ('trill call' BWP), consisting of a brief fast trill on 3 or 4 quite shrill, thin notes, like clipped versions of the call at 78. Note the similar timbre, though higher-pitched than the **Cirl Bunting** song following.

Bonelli's Warbler song consists of an even, regular trill, but typically less than 1 second in length, so much shorter than Cirl Bunting, though at around the same speed. The up-slurred notes, so different in form from the previous trills, also give the trill a liquid bubbling quality, rather distinct from insect-like rattling of Cirl Bunting songs. Note the less regular pattern in the song-type of the second example (from the same bird, recorded a little later) and the Cirl Bunting songs in the background. The bird in the example is probably of the western species; BWP reports eastern (orientalis) birds' songs as slower and quieter.

Wood Warbler songs feature a more elaborate trill, which builds to a resolved crescendo, and are pretty unmistakable; but the similarity to Bonelli's Warbler is noticeable, with an exaggerated liquid sibilance at the start becoming relatively more rattling in the second half. Wood Warbler's song is higher-pitched and has more high-frequency energy (sibilance) than Bonelli's. Since the two species are congeneric and occur sympatrically, they make an interesting case study for species song recognition criteria; see Catchpole & Slater for a brief discussion on the results of early playback experiments by J.C.Bremond on the qualities of song that turn on a Bonelli's Warbler. The repeated, plaintive note between the trills is also regarded as part of the song or an alternative song, but is given less frequently than the trill; the usual call is a very similar note (cf. 87).

For other rattling trills listen to the calls of Redpoll at 93, Greenfinch at 89,

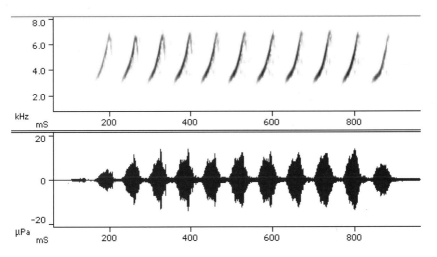

Fig. 18 Bonelli's Warbler song (46, 0'09").

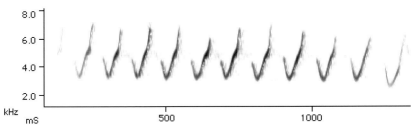

Fig. 19 Bonelli's Warbler song (46, 0'26").

and the more sibilant trills in pipit songs at 66 and 67; other cardueline finches produce a variety of trills in their songs, and remember Nuthatch has a sustained, even, trilling song.

Jangling trills 47

Corn Bunting, Serin

Although not normally thought of as a trill, **Corn Bunting** male song is a series of repeated hard notes, with the rate of repetition quickly accelerating to a speed where separate notes are inaudible, then slowing down briefly to an ending; the notes have an insect (stridulation) quality, similar to Cirl and Yellowhammer, but the varied, rapid repetition gives the over-all jangling quality often referred to. This makes an interesting song to playback at half-speed or slower if you have the facilities. Much research has been done on variations in Corn Bunting song-types in Britain and France by Dr Peter McGregor and the Behaviour & Ecology Research Group at Nottingham University. Groups of adjacent males have been found to share song-types, differing from other groups on a microgeographic scale (e.g. 3 groups within a 15 km distance); the mosaic pattern of clumped variation on this sort of scale is at the root of the idea of local dialects. Separate populations of a species showing differing song-types are a different case.

Despite the complex patterning of pitch variation in the fast warble, **Serin** song has a fairly unique thin jangling quality ('jingle as from glass splinters' LJ), similar in timbre to Corn Bunting. The usual flight call is a short, 'sisisit'-like, trilled phrase in a similar voice.

Tinkling trills   49

Waxwing, Greenfinch

Waxwings are generally quite vocal in their winter flocks; calls have a soft bell-like tone unlike the main calls of any other British species. These calls may be delivered with variable intensity, from soft, barely audible contact calls among the members of a flock, rising in intensity if birds become more agitated, through to the full voice of an alarm call. During the last two winters several Waxwing flocks passed through our village; I suspect they lingered no longer than a day or two, yet I kept hearing that tinkling trill on odd occasions in gardens several hundred yards away. Further investigation revealed the source as **Greenfinch**; at a distance the other trills were merging with other sounds but I was picking up the tinkling trills. Are the phrases generally common among Greenfinches in other areas? I have not had the chance of finding out. Is it a sound that some Greenfinch groups have appropriated through brief association with these exotic visitors?

Wheezing trills   50

Brambling, Greenfinch

Brambling song is typically a Greenfinch-like wheeze with a characteristic, slightly nasal resonance; rare variants have been reported (LJ). The energy is concentrated between 3 kHz and 4 kHz and the pitch is held there through-

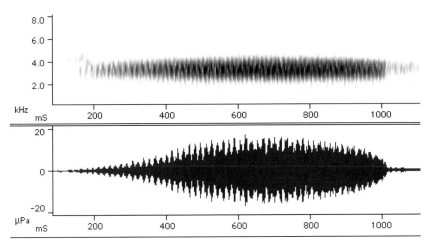

Fig. 20 Brambling song (50, 0'20").

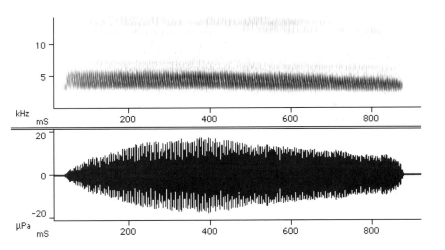

Fig. 21 Greenfinch song (50, 0'32").

out. The Brambling's song builds more gradually to its peak than Green-finch, which is noticeable if you compare the dynamic envelope in the waveform with that of the Greenfinch. **Greenfinch** 'dzwee'-type song is slightly higher-pitched and has more high-frequency harmonic emphasis (giving the sibilant buzzing quality); its crescendo comes quicker, then there is a gradual slight fade and lowering of pitch.

Locustella warbler songs 51

Grasshopper Warbler, Savi's Warbler, River Warbler, Bushcricket species

This genus of Warblers has been named from the orthopteran-like songs of the European species (some species from the Eastern Palaearctic do not have such songs). Not only are they fairly plain 'little brown jobs', they are skulking in behaviour, generally obscured by the rank, damp vegetation used for summer habitat in Northern Europe.

Grasshopper Warbler has streaking on back (though the contrast may be light) and light streaking on breast. Song is often delivered from near the top of rank vegetation or part-way up a shrub if available, with the bird not quite out in the open, frequently at night and twilight, but can also be heard at any time of day. Note the composition of the reel in the waveform: the rate of around 24 double notes per second is considerably slower than Savi's at around 50 per second.

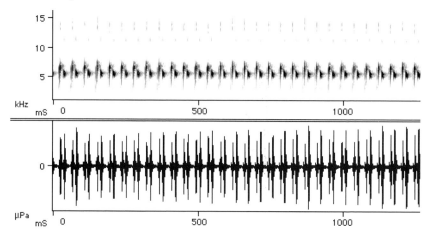

Fig. 22 Grasshopper Warbler – part of song (51, 0'10").

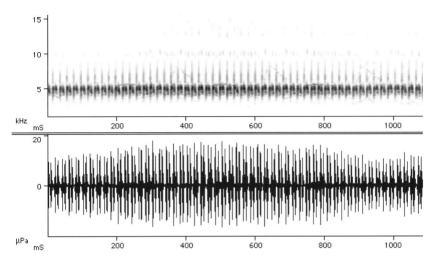

Fig. 23 Savi's Warbler – part of song (52, 0'15").

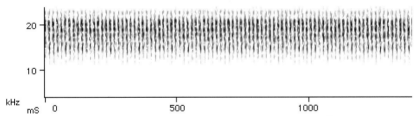

Fig. 24 Roesel's Bushcricket – part of song (not on CD). The energy is at a much higher frequency.

Savi's Warbler has plainer plumage (confusable with Reed Warbler), is a bulkier bird and tends more to reed beds. Song may be delivered from exposed positions, such as the top of a reed or a willow bush and Simms described the species as less shy than Grasshopper Warbler. The example of song given features an unusually long burst and the species is generally regarded to sing in shorter bursts than Grasshopper. The accelerating 'tik's that start up the song are distinctive. Although the differences in pitch and timbre between these two species are easy to detect in comparison, it is more difficult when faced with a single reeling bird in the field.

Burton and Johnson (also cited in Macmillan) point out the similarity of

Savi's song to the stridulation of Roesel's Bush-cricket *Metrioptera roeselii*, which is continuous and buzzing. In Britain Roesel's Bush-cricket has a fairly restricted, though expanding, distribution and is not heard singing before maturity in July, though up to a month earlier in mainland Europe. I find the sound distinctively thinner and high-pitched.

The CD includes the song of an unidentified orthopteran species in Southern France, which I found confusing, when looking for Savi's Warbler; but note the short, even bursts.

River Warbler generally resembles Savi's, with plain back plumage, but features some light streaking to the breast, and light edges to the under-tail coverts; its habitat preferences tend more towards Grasshopper Warbler. Song has a shuffling rhythm, quite distinct from the even reels of those species. Burton and Johnson list a number of Bush-crickets whose songs are similar to River Warbler, and several Cicadas

Acrocephalus warbler songs   54

Reed Warbler, Marsh Warbler, Sedge Warbler, Cetti's Warbler

Acrocephalus warblers tend towards longish, more or less continuous bouts of singing: Reed at an even pace and level intensity, but both Marsh and Sedge's songs tend to vary in pace, building and subsiding in intensity. The period of full song tends to be short in the *Acrocephalus* warblers, particularly Marsh Warbler

The example of **Reed Warbler** features two adjacent males singing simultaneously - hence the intensity. Songs are typically composed of repetitive phrases of short squeaking, chirping and grating-trilled notes, delivered at a throbbing, even pace and pitch and sometimes including mimicry, but rarely to the extent or fluency of Marsh Warbler. Singers tend to remain in cover, rarely rising to the top of the reeds. From what I have heard, apart from the introductory Nightingale-like notes, the song of Moustached Warbler sounds very similar to Reed Warbler.

Marsh Warbler song is marked by variation in both pace and phrases, often beginning hesitantly with a single repeated note (a Chiffchaff-like call in the example) building into quick-fire sequences of trills, wheezes and mimicked calls. The particular kind of trills and nasal wheezes are distinctive once heard. The species is famous for its mimicry; Simms reports from the studies of F. Dowsett-Lemaire that, of a total of 212 recorded species-imitations, 133 were of species from the African autumn and winter grounds; the

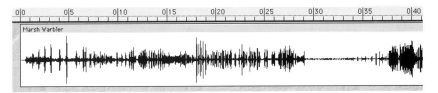

Fig. 25 Marsh Warbler song (55, 0'05") waveform of about 40 seconds. In continuous passages, but irregular. The scale at the top is in minutes and seconds. Compare the structures with the Nightingales and the Shrike later.

average individual repertoire of species imitated was around 76. Blythe's Reed Warbler's song can sound very similar to Marsh Warbler.

This **Sedge Warbler** song features the buzzing or slightly grating, trilled notes so characteristic of the species and typical halting rhythm changes - trying a bit too hard to be jazz. This includes what sounds like imitations of Swallow and Willow Warbler; many songs include longer passages of mimicry than in this example, but less elaborate and more repetitive than Marsh Warbler and usually interspersed with buzzing motifs.

Cetti's Warbler song is obvious in its form - a loud explosive outburst. In voice and style the phrases could be part of a Marsh Warbler song, but Cetti's repeat the same stereotyped song at long intervals (the interval was edited down from over 20 seconds in the example, and longer intervals are frequent). It is typically a single explosive note followed by a pause, introducing several (2-3) repetitive phrases of short syllables. Songs are stereotyped but differ between individuals who will change to a different and distinct song type in response to a territorial challenge (Luschi & Del Seppia, 1996, *Ibis*, 138, 479-484)

Eric Simms in *British Warblers* gives full coverage on voice to all the British species, including accidentals.

Luscinia spp & Red-backed Shrike songs   57

Nightingale, Thrush Nightingale, Bluethroat, Winchat, Red-backed Shrike

The three species of the *Luscinia* genus covered here might on casual listening appear to have very loose song structures, but this is largely an illusion created by the large repertoires of phrases, which get used in different combinations. For a full analysis of the difference between Thrush Nightingale and Nightingale song see BWP. With these species it is interest-

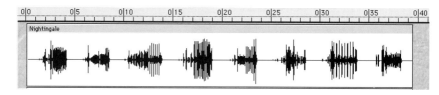

Fig. 26 Nightingale song (57).

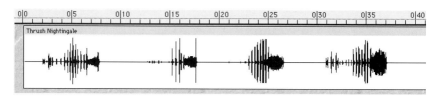

Fig. 27 Thrush Nightingale song (58, 0'04").

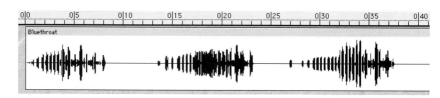

Fig. 28 Bluethroat song (59, 0'05").

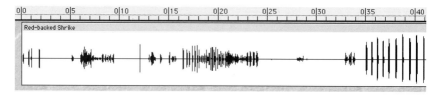

Fig. 29 Red-backed Shrike song (60, 0'05").

ing to take an overview of a period of singing. These waveforms are of the first 40 seconds of the respective recordings, showing the different dynamic structures.

This **Nightingale** example features a particularly high rate of song with short, regular gaps; in other instances of song the gaps are often longer; the length and dynamics of the song strophes are typical for full song. Compare the Nightingale song on the NSA CD for songs closer to Thrush Nightingale in both form and phrases, with some unusually long trills. In contrast each Nightingale song is typically shorter over-all (except ones that begin with series of rising whistled 'pew's), at a faster pace, rises more quickly to a crescendo level in the middle with more varied phrases and longer (rapid-fire) repetitions; endings are often a single high or rising note.

Thrush Nightingale song is typically at a slower pace, rising more gradually from the introductory notes (usually clear, sad whistles), to a few deliberate repetitions (often hollow 'tchoks') and usually with an extended rattle leading up to the terminal note. Each strophe is generally longer than in Nightingale (up to twice as long - BWP). But note that on occasions birds may sing at a quicker pace and deliver songs with briefer intros, sounding much more like a Nightingale than the bird in this example; familiarity with a number of different singers helps in getting a feel for the differences. The two clips of rasping elements at the end sound like the 'rattling phrase' and the 'castanet phrase' referred to in BWP. Note the interrupted song and low alarm croak at 0'50".

Bluethroat songs begin hesitantly, but with typical *Luscinia* accelerating repetitions, usually a mimicked note (the first song in the example a Swallow- or Wagtail-like note, the second a Greenfinch-like one); the song gradually builds up momentum before entering a free-form section, with varied trills and buzzy scratchings (like Wheatear or Black Redstart cf. 44). Note the thinner, higher-pitched voice compared to the previous two nightingales and the bell-like tone of some of the notes; in some songs this is more marked than in the example. Birds in full song may extend strophes into more or less continuous passages. Compare the songs of Marsh Warbler (55) and Red-backed Shrike (66) for over-all structure and the kind of notes and phrases they voice. A short extract follows from a Scottish **Winchat** that had me wondering briefly if it was a Bluethroat.

Red-backed Shrike male song is marked by its mimicry, the often stuttering, constant rhythmic variation and lack of any overall structure, giving an impression of meandering warbles in a rather thin, sometimes scratchy voice. The more flowing phrases may be comparable to Bluethroat or Marsh Warbler, but they often merge into a chattering, caricature of the subject. Blackbird, Meadow Pipit, Chaffinch and Skylark are all covered here - you may pick up some others. The Sparrow-like chirps at 0'40" and the Snipe-like scarps at 0'37" seem to be the advertising call (2a) and 'chee-uk' call (2b) respectively, referred to in BWP.

Finch songs 61

Scarlet Rosefinch, Crossbill

Scarlet Rosefinch male song is a stereotyped repetition unusual in the finches, slightly reminiscent of an Ortolan Bunting, but more lively; the simple three or four note form and the whistling tone with slurred pitching are the distinctive features. Different song types can be expressed 'see-teuy-teuy-cheew' (as in the example) and 'weete-woyte-wehu'. LJ records that some males may give a twitter between phrases. The other, Brambling-like, wheezy calls in the recording may be from a Northern Bullfinch seen in the tree at the same time; but with parabolic reflector recording there is always the possibility of the microphone picking up a more distant, unnoticed bird that is right on the central axis (cf. Sound Pictures on p.16 for a sonogram of the last song).

Whereas a strictly-defined full song of a male **Crossbill** may be quite a rare occurrence, snatches of song can be heard for much of the year - the social and breeding behavioural patterns are unusual and complex in this species. Hence it is a useful species to be able to identify in the coniferous symphony, so to speak. The tone of voice is distinctive and is similar to the species' calls. It has characteristically ringing, slightly metallic chirps, trills and purer notes, varying in loudness; in form birds sing fairly continuously, but with some more hesitant passages and pauses, repeating particular short motifs several times, but working-in some variations. The example given is part of a full male song lasting 5 mins; note the Bullfinch-like warbling, almost subsong passage towards the end. Like so many species, an under-rated musician.

My Crossbill guru tells me that there are variations in call voicing between different Crossbill groups, but that evidence is lacking for a distinct song from Scottish-type birds. I have been told that birds of the Scottish type crop up in Northumberland and Wales, which confuses the issue just a little too much for me.

Upland passerine songs 63

Snow Bunting, Lapland Bunting, Shore Lark

I find the male songs of these three species confusingly similar: the songs are usually around 1 to 3 seconds long and often composed of slurred notes, voiced with a slightly dry, creaky or wheezing tone characteristic of the buntings, though Shorelark is from an unrelated family (and has a hint of the more liquid, chirping tone of Skylark, but see below). All three species perform song flights, when, at least with Lapland Bunting and Shorelark, it seems song may be more continuous. Fortunately for most of us, our interest lies less in separating the three species from each other by song, and more in differentiating their songs from other more common upland species such as Meadow Pipit, Skylark or Wheatear.

Snow Bunting song probably features the most stereotyped repetition. It tends to be simpler in form and delivered at a lively pace, with whistling, pitch-swept phrases reminiscent of Scarlet Rosefinch; there is a more even emphasis on all notes and often a phrase is repeated within a song (though Lapland Bunting songs may feature this as well). Two examples are given, the first from Scotland, the second from Scandinavia, but both birds are singing very similar song types; the Icelandic bird in the example on the NSA CD differs more from these two. Desmond Nethersole-Thompson, who studied the Scottish birds earlier this century, reports that birds of both races were involved: *nivalis* with white-rumped males (Scandinavia and Greenland) and *insulae* with dark-rumped males (Iceland). According to BWP, local dialects are a feature with this species and they quote Nethersole-Thompson's report that the Inuit used these dialects to navigate in dense fog - a case of applied ornithomusicology! Nevertheless in recent research on Spitzbergen reported in Bioacoustics (Y. Espmark, 1995, *Bioacoustics*, 6, 117-133), all except one of 24 male Snow Buntings were found to have only one song type, which differed between birds, and no evidence was found to support the occurrence of local dialects. Hmm.

In contrast **Lapland Bunting** male song is typically slightly longer and more elaborate in structure, with more notes, and may be delivered at a more relaxed pace with slurred phrases featuring harmonically complex notes and little trills; songs give more of a jingling impression than those of Snow

Fig. 30 Snow Bunting song (63, 0'37")

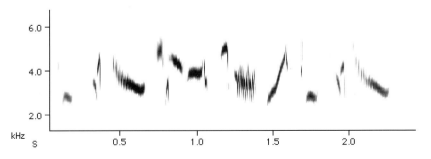

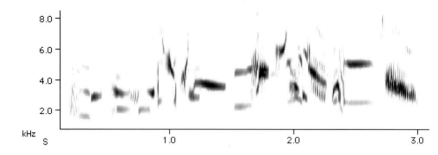

Fig. 31 Lapland Bunting song (64, 0'32"), showing more complex harmonic structures.

Bunting. Thorpe suggests that the complexity (and repetitiveness) of Lapland Bunting song (in comparison to other Emberizidae) is probably an adaptation to aerial singing; I believe the songs in the two examples are from perched birds, but another of John Corbett's recordings, taken during a butterfly-like, hovering display-flight, was if anything a more stereotyped, simpler repetition at regular intervals of a song no different in style to those in the examples given. Birds on breeding territory often call persistently, alternating two Bullfinch-like notes (similar in sound to some of the calls at the beginning of these examples) (rendered 'dyuee' and 'triu' by LJ) at monotonously regular intervals.

In this example of **Shorelark** song, subsequent strophes vary a little, but are typically a lazy repeated note accelerating to a slight crescendo - note the lilting pitch. The example of songflight in JCR is a hesitantly continuous

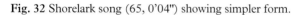

Fig. 32 Shorelark song (65, 0'04") showing simpler form.

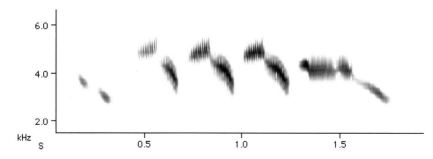

twittering more akin to skylark than the example here; the second example of calls given in JCR bears some similarity to the vocalisations here and may be subsong or plastic phase of song. The description of male song in BWP, though possibly applicable to the example in JCR, does not fit the example given here very well; it also points out that song is thought to differ slightly in Eastern races and this seems to be the case with this Turkish bird.

Pipit songs 66

Meadow Pipit, Tree Pipit

The full singing behaviour of these 2 species is typical of the genus, where a series of songs from a prominent perch alternates with a longer song delivered in a parachuting display flight. **Meadow Pipit** tends to sing from a perch between ground- and shrub-height and usually sings during the ascent in its display flight; Tree Pipit tends to sing from a higher perch in trees up to medium-height and usually makes a fluttering ascent in its display flight before beginning the song. The perched songs and the first part of the song flight of Meadow Pipit are slow, but gradually accelerating, repetitions of a single note, 'tsu' or 'tchi'; during the descent of the display flight the song changes to one or more trills on different notes, sometimes including Tree Pipit-like wheezes. In the examples given, the first song is from a bird perched on a clump of heather, the second from the same bird in a rather short display flight and the third is the second half of a display flight from a different bird.

Tree Pipit perched songs tend to be shorter than in display flight, but are nearly always composed of several distinct trills, and break straight into a sprightly Chaffinch-like trill. In fact the whole of the first song in the examples given is very Chaffinch-like; the second, also a perched song has a different, more typically Tree Pipit ending and subsequent perched songs generally have varied final phrases. The third song, from the same bird but not consequent to the first two, was recorded during a display flight to a more distant tree; the slowing-down repetitions of an extended note are fairly typical (especially 'seea-seea-seea').

The Chaffinch-like feel of the opening phrases is common and results in the species being easily overlooked where there are numerous Chaffinches singing. Redstart male songs often have a similar opening phrase. Rock Pipit songs are closer to Meadow Pipit in form, but with a harder 'tch'-type note.

Marsh, Willow & Crested tits 68

Marsh Tit, Willow Tit, Coal Tit, Blue Tit, Great Tit, Reed Bunting,
Crested Tit, Goldcrest, Coal Tit

Coal, Great and Blue Tits are readily identified visually; nevertheless familiarity with the voices of these species is essential for a good working knowledge of woodland sounds, since they are such vocal species and comprise
such a large proportion of woodland vocal activity. The visual distinctions
between Marsh and Willow Tits on the other hand are very fine and a matter
of degree; the usual calls and songs of the two species, though variable,
provide a more reliable or additional distinction. The rattling trill of Crested
Tit is useful for simply locating the species.

The rather explosive, down-slurred, clear 'zing' (sibilant compared to the
ringing Coal Tit) in the first syllable of the 'pitchou' call of **Marsh Tit**
(sometimes given by itself) is the most distinctive aspect; when it is extended
to 'pitchou-chu-chu-chu' (Macmillan) the 'chu-chu-chu' has a similar nasal
timbre to the 'tchay' call of the Willow Tit. The repeated 'tchay' calls are at
a slower rate, with each call an emphatic separate syllable compared to the
more fluent 'chu-chu-chu's of Marsh Tit.

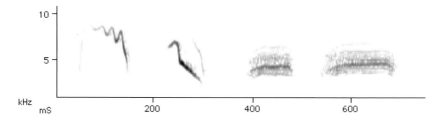

Fig. 33 Marsh Tit call (68, 0'12").

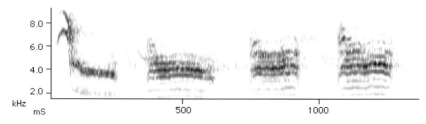

Fig. 34 Willow Tit call (69, 0'06").

50

Willow Tit often has a thin note or two to introduce the calls ('si-zur-zur-zur' in Macmillan), but this has a slightly wheezy timbre that characterises Willow's calls in contrast to Marsh. The call in the third example was recorded soon after the previous one; the bird was not seen but suspected to be a juvenile Willow. The calls in the last example seemed to be from a

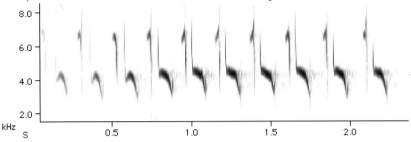

Fig. 35 Marsh Tit song (70, 0'04").

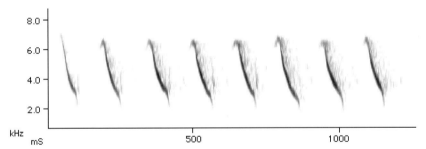

Fig. 36 Marsh Tit song (70, 0'16").

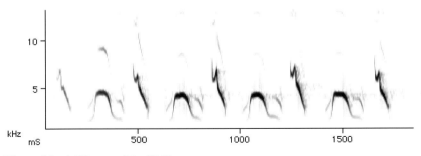

Fig. 37 Marsh Tit song (70, 0'20").

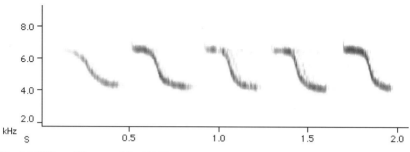

Fig. 38 Willow Tit song (71, 0'13")

family party and probably feature the descending 'jzee-jzee-jzee' begging call of young referred to in Macmillan.

In the **Blue Tit** example a number of birds seemed to be feeding and courting in early spring as they moved through a wood that had been empty the week before. The **Great Tits** seemed to be in a family party and sound alarmed, though I did not see why.

The usual songs of Marsh and Willow are distinct enough, but the varied song-types of Marsh Tit and more unusual songs of Willow (including a fast, trilling 'warble', possibly the 'zi-ze zerrl' of LJ) can be rather confusing; and Willow Tit is thought to sing infrequently for a *Parus* tit (BWP). **Marsh Tit** songs tend to be fast repetitions of one or two notes with a chiming quality akin to Great Tit songs; in the fourth example the bird was in the early, experimental or plastic phase of song.

Willow Tit songs are typically 3 to 5 repetitions of a down-slurred almost disyllabic element at a slower rate than Marsh, 'siu-siu-siu' (LJ), comparable to the 'pew'-type song of Wood Warbler (cf. 46).

The **Great Tit** song has the right over-all form (and had me fooled until it changed song-type), but the **Reed Bunting** call is closer in the timbre and form of the elements. The notes of the songs of the alpine populations of Willow Tit in Central Europe are not down-inflected (BWP). In sum classic vocalisations of Willow and Marsh Tits are distinctive, but both species also give a range of calls and songs that are much less so (cf. JCR for further variations on both species).

Crested Tit are a fairly vocal species whose calls are a mix of high-pitched, thin 'zee'-type calls, with a shriller edge than Goldcrest, and the more distinctive purring or rattling trill; both types of call can be heard in the examples, but note there are other species calling in the first example. The trills have a slightly squeaky hardness, not really apparent in the calls of

Goldcrest and **Coal Tit** in the following examples (note that they are in this order and **not** as announced on the CD).

Crested warbler songs 73

Goldcrest, Firecrest

Goldcrest songs build on a repetition of a rhythmic motif with a melodic pattern (pitch modulation) before emerging with a fast, warbled phrase for an ending; this makes it easier to appreciate differing song types in this species than with Firecrest. Note how the voicing is fuller in the subsong example than in other Goldcrest vocalisations, becoming more tit-like.

Firecrest song is a rhythmic intensification of essentially a single repeated element, which appears to become slightly shriller and rise in pitch; some songs can feature a few differently pitched notes, but never with the more elaborate patterning of Goldcrest. Notice the acceleration in Firecrest song; it is probably most similar to the rhythmically varied calling of excited Goldcrests. Firecrest calls are in a similar voice to its song, with a sharper,

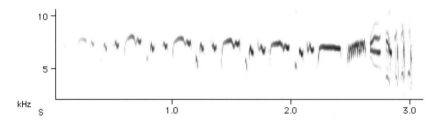

Fig. 39 Goldcrest song (73, 0'16").

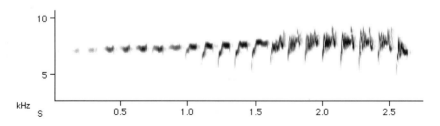

Fig. 40 Firecrest song (74, 0'20")

slightly metallic timbre and lacking in the trilling sibilance in contrast with Goldcrest.

High thin 'see' calls   75

Goldcrest, Long-tailed Tit, Treecreeper, Robin, Dunnock, Kingfisher, Spotted Flycatcher, Song Thrush, Blackbird, Redwing, Fieldfare

Many small passerine species have thin, high-pitched 'see'-type contact calls, usually short and not particularly loud; this includes all the tit species, including Long-tailed, Treecreeper and Nuthatch: I find it impossible to distinguish more than a hint of species characteristics in these calls by ear. Many small passerine species also have similar, very thin-sounding, high-pitched and slightly down-slurred, alarm calls that are difficult to locate because of these acoustic characteristics; these are difficult to identify to species, though differing slightly, but worth picking up on as potential raptor alerts. (For further reading on these calls and sound localisation see Catchpole & Slater, p.88, or Thorpe, p.30). Here we concentrate on the difficult, but more distinctive and louder, high-pitched, thin contact calls frequently heard

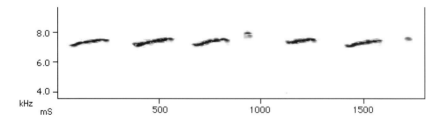

Fig. 41 Goldcrest calls (75, 0'11").

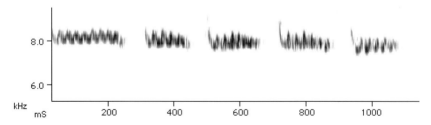

Fig. 42 Goldcrest calls (75, 0'38").

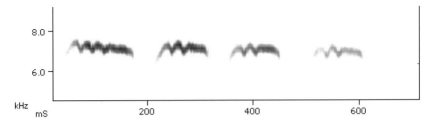

Fig. 43 Long-tailed Tit calls (76, 0'09").

from a number of species. The first group are often heard together in mixed flocks from autumn through the winter and provide a challenge for the ear.

Goldcrests tend to group outside the breeding season and are generally vocal even when foraging; this is even more true of Long-tailed Tits. Goldcrest calls can be very variable in length and patterns of delivery, but generally in a thin, quite pure, high voice, sometimes slightly trilled (especially when excited, such as in parties approaching roosting); towards Spring, calling may include warbled phrases at a lower pitch (cf. subsong at 73).

Long-tailed Tits use several more distinctive calls such as the terse 'tchup' and soft trill; but also typically a descending 'see-see-see(-see)' at a brisk pace, and these calls carry further than the former. Though easily confused with Goldcrest, the particular pattern of delivery is distinctive, as is the relatively clear and only slightly trilled sibilance.

Treecreepers frequently associate with the previous two species in winter flocks, but often at a little distance from the centre of activity. Birds call frequently while foraging with a very soft, terse 'see', or 'swit' heard closely (after the long calls in the example), which may be a clue to their presence, but is not easily distinguished from similar calls from a number of species and does not carry far. Longer distance contact calls, the louder calls in the example, are given at longer intervals, frequently at the start or end of working a tree. These are usually a series of up to a dozen, or more, even, extended notes, with little variation to the pitch, though heavily-trilled, and delivered at fairly long intervals.

The hard-to-locate alarm call of **Robin** follows; notice how thin, but piercing it sounds. These calls have sometimes been called aerial predator alarms, as distinct from ground predator, but in encounters with Robin, Blackbird and Dunnock (including the recording here) the birds appeared to be calling at my intrusion. Possibly they are used in any situation where a bird does not want to draw attention to itself.

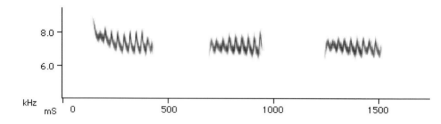

Fig. 44 Treecreeper calls (77, 0'08").

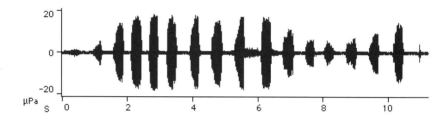

Fig. 45 Treecreeper calls (77, 0'06") waveform of 10 seconds.

In contrast to the previous calls of this section, the general contact and alarm call of **Dunnock** is a fuller-sounding 'tsuu' ('seeh' LJ), with a distinct, slightly sibilant whistling timbre. Note the length and slightly abrupt delivery. In contrast the calls of **Kingfisher** have a subtly different sibilance, are slightly down-slurred with a faded ending; but are nevertheless easily confused. Contact calls of **Spotted Flycatcher** have lost the pure whistling quality of the previous calls and are marked by an emphatic, but irregular, slightly squeaky, trilling quality. **Robin** has several types of call that might be rendered 'tsee'. Several have a slightly sustained, loose trill like the previous species, as in the first and third examples; the calls in the second example are more abrupt with a clear, ringing timbre suggesting the alarm call 4 in BWP, but the calls were from a bird gathering nesting material and showing no outward signs of unease.

The terse, rather explosive 'tsip' ('tic' in LJ) of **Song Thrush** is the usual call given in flight, particularly by migrants on the move; it is a useful call to recognise and easily overlooked. The equivalent call from **Blackbird** is usually a fuller, sustained note with an emphatic sibilant trill, but is quite variable and can sound closer to Redwing than the version in the example. **Redwing** contact calls are very similar to those of Blackbird, but have a thinner and purer, zinging trill in contrast, 'tseurr' or 'zeep' (Macmillan); these are the calls heard at night from migrants in autumn and, like the previous species, individuals' calls vary. The sharp single 'jeks' in the example ('kuk' LJ) are another commonly-used call. In contrast **Fieldfare** contact calls are usually in chuckling runs made up of distinctly squelchy-sounding notes. The vocabulary of Fieldfares is quite complex and includes squeals, nasal notes and a high thin 'see' from birds on migration, but less often heard. Blackbird 'chuk'-type calls are variable in intensity and several distinct types are recognised by BWP; from softer percussive warning calls, through the medium intensity alarm calls in the example to the repeated metallic 'chink's often heard at roosting time. Likewise **Song Thrush** warning and alarm calls vary from sharp 'tuk's or 'djuk's (BWP) to rapid-fire bursts of 'tschi's in full alarm (both in the example).

Sharp 'tic' calls 82

Hawfinch, Robin, Redstart, Black Redstart, Blackcap, Winchat, Wheatear, Stonechat, Wren, Great Spotted Woodpecker

'Tic', 'tch' and 'chak'-type calls, percussive and harmonically-rich, are more easily located to their source by ear and often function as distracting alarm calls (cf. the high-pitched, thin alarm call of Robin, 78); such calls also tend to be used by passerines for mobbing the likes of Tawny Owls. With many species, such as Hawfinch and Robin, they also seem to serve as more general contact calls and, in the case of Hawfinch, feature heavily in singing. The calls from Redstart, Black Redstart, Blackcap, Winchat, Wheatear and Stonechat are all alarm calls caused by my presence in their breeding territories.

Hawfinch 'tzic' calls vary in volume and although in general contact they may not be heard at any distance, given as alarm calls or in flight they may be audible for several hundred metres in quieter conditions. In the examples given, a flock of about 12 birds were scattered in several groups around some yew trees. In the brighter intervals of a blustery morning they were starting to court a little with this sort of subsong and a couple of birds occasionally dashed off on a chase through the wood. Full advertising or territorial song is not very marked in Hawfinches, but in courtship softer song like this may be quite frequent yet remain inaudible to observers at any distance (cf. G. Mountfort, *The Hawfinch*, p63). Note the explosive sibilance in comparison to the 'tic' calls of **Robin** following; the three examples given are from different birds and show some of the variability in both timbre and patterns of delivery. The 'tic' calls of **Redstart** are similar to Robin, but slightly richer and fuller, though not loud.

The similar calls of **Black Redstart** are still very abrupt, but are approaching those of Blackcap in harmonic richness, with a distinct, percussive timbre. The alternating 'swee'-type call is probably the same as that expressed as 'sip' in BWP (4a), where it is said to be the only call in winter and often given in series. Both male and female are calling in the example.

In comparison the 'tchk' call of **Blackcap** is fuller, slightly longer and more emphatically delivered; BWP distinguishes two versions of this call, a general contact-alarm call and a more intense alarm-warning call (the softer call heard seems to be the mewing sound referred to). Several other *Sylvia* warblers have very similar calls, including Lesser and Common Whitethroats. The 'tch' call of **Winchat** is terse, rather softer and usually accompanied by rich 'suu'-type calls reminiscent of Bullfinch ('fiu' and 'tec-tec' in BWP). The similar call of **Wheatear** is a harder, more rattling 'chak', of slightly longer duration, accompanied in the example by thin, penetrating 'seep' calls which are often heard alone ('tuc' and 'weet' in BWP). **Stonechat** calls, often transcribed as 'chack' (BWP) or 'tsak' (HFP), are clearly in this example a more buzzing, rattle, also slightly longer than the similar calls of previous species and closer to the 'trak' of LJ (compare also with the Sedge Warbler alarm call at 42); the accompanying warning call is a noticeably sharp, abrupt, thin whistle - 'weet'.

And finally two examples of sharp 'tk' **Wren** alarm calls and an example of the fuller 'tchik' of **Great Spotted Woodpecker** are given for comparison.

Many other species from various families have similar 'tak'- or 'chk'-type calls, including many of the *Locustella*, *Acrocephalus* and *Hippolais* warblers, Dusky Warbler, some of the *Parus* tit species, Long-tailed Tit and Spotted Flycatcher.

'Hooeet' & 'teu' type calls 85

Willow Warbler, Redstart, Chiffchaff, Chaffinch, Nightingale, Great Tit, Wood Warbler, Siskin, Coal Tit.

The disyllabic 'hoo-eet' of **Willow Warbler** is a sweet-toned whistle and according to BWP is rarely heard in the spring but is usually the only call heard from the species after June when song has passed. The first example is of a family party, with other birds calling in the distance, but also with a

Wood Warbler giving its contact and alarm call (cf. 87). The similar call of **Redstart** is less mellow, more shrill, shorter and more abrupt; the call is also given with the 'tic' calls by the bird at 82.

In contrast the similar call from **Chiffchaff** is a single, slurred, more piercing syllable with a hint of wheezy squeal, better rendered 'wheet' (or 'hweet' as in BWP). The following 2 examples were recorded from different birds on the same September morning at a river-side site, with scrub and woodland, about 5 miles inland; good numbers of Chiffchaffs turn up here and several sites nearby in September, and call variants are as common as standard calls. Although the thin 'sweeoo' might suggest one of the eastern races *abietinus* or *tristis* (cf. HFP) and the simple 'weep' might suggest the monosyllabic 'peep' of *tristis* (cf. Macmillan), I think they are more likely to be variant calls of *collybita* and western *abietinus* (cf. BWP). The Macmillan Guide also refers to a squeakier, more monosyllabic call for juvenile Willow Warblers. Note also that Spanish Chiffchaffs (*ibericus* race) have songs somewhere between *collybita* Chiffchaffs and Willow Warblers.

The 'weet' call of **Chaffinch** ('huit', 'hreet' and 'breeze' in BWP) is a much briefer, sound and usually delivered in regular repetition (more so than in the example), sometimes as doubles. This call varies from the fairly pure whistle in the example, to more churred versions and has also been referred to as the rain call. **Nightingale** alarm calls are very similar to the previous Chaffinch call, but are purer in tone, have a less emphatic rise in pitch and are delivered to a more nervous rhythm; the croak is diagnostic but, unlike the whistled note, does not carry for any distance. This **Great Tit** call, which is generally common in Northumberland, can be deceptive; at a distance the 'see' gets lost but the 'huee' still rings out, suggesting Willow Warbler or Redstart.

The **Wood Warbler** call is very similar to the repeated note used as an alternative song and has been variously transcribed as 'pew' (Macmillan), 'tiuh' (LJ) and 'puu' (HFP); the version in the example is a fairly pure, low whistle without a fast, down-slurred opening, but with a sustained even pitch (cf. the song at 46); the delivery is often deliberate, with regular repetition, as in the example. **Coal Tit** 'teu'-type contact calls are variable in voicing from a short 'tee' or 'tu', to a more extended 'teuy' (almost disyllabic and rising in pitch like a Willow Warbler 'hooeet') and frequently as a double note 'teuy-ti'; the calls are thinner and higher-pitched than Wood Warbler, but ring out well in woodland. **Siskin** 'teu' calls ring out like those of Coal Tit, but are less varied in both voicing and pitch and have something more of the plaintiveness of Wood Warbler. Heard at close range, the voice often has a slight wheeziness, which becomes more pronounced in the accompanying 'turlee's ('sweeeloo' in Macmillan) and chattering notes. The calls in the example are from several birds flying into the tops of some birch trees; a Wren gives its 'tch' alarm call several times at the beginning (cf. also 92 for more examples of Siskin alarm and contact calls).

Finch contact calls 88

Brambling, Chaffinch, Bullfinch, Greenfinch, Crossbill, Linnet, Twite, Goldfinch, Siskin, Redpoll

The usual call given in flight by the finches is the general contact and alarm 'teu'- or 'chip'-type syllable and is usually easy for a tuned-in ear to identify, but variation within species can be confusing.

In contrast with the analogous calls of Chaffinch with whom they often flock, **Brambling** 'chuc' (HFP), 'yup' (LJ) or 'tsuk' calls have a wheezy timbre akin to Linnet and Twite, but not the percussiveness or twang of those two species; the calls have an understated softness similar to Chaffinch's, though the force of delivery can vary, and are the usual calls given in flight. The 'dzwee' calls ('wheezing eeehp' in LJ) also given in the example are distinctive, with a much fuller voicing than anything similar from Linnet, Twite or Chaffinch.

The contact calls that **Chaffinches** usually use in flight are subtly variable and interpretations include 'chiff', 'tsup' (HFP) and 'tupe' (BWP); typically the call is short, mellow in tone and often repeated but not in rhythmic patterns. The note can have something of the wooden, percussiveness of Greenfinch and on another occasion something of the explosive squeak of Crossbill (and because of similar calling patterns, may be confusing).

The usual calls heard from **Bullfinch** are very similar to the previous calls in timbre, but are usually lower in pitch and, because they are sustained longer (though still short notes), sound fuller-bodied and harmonically richer. BWP recognises a number of different categories of these 'teu' or 'phew' calls and points out that Bullfinches have a complex repertoire with at least 17 distinct calls. The bird in the first example was thought to be a juvenile, but the bird in the second was an adult - the third example is the same bird. The calls in the third example are rather quiet and easily overlooked (the playback level has been increased here); the bird is actually giving two calls - the higher-pitched 'chiff' and the soft whistle. Calls given in flight are sometimes typical Bullfinch 'teu's and sometimes more Chaffinch-like notes.

Greenfinch calls are based on a clipped note, 'chip' or 'tu', varying from the rather Chaffinch-like, but lower-pitched and richer calls of the first two examples to the more wooden notes in the runs of the following example. The first two may be from juveniles, since both adults and juveniles were present. The short trilled runs of very clipped notes are characteristic and familiar, but note the slower runs in flight in the last example.

Crossbill contact calls are a clipped note similar to Greenfinch, but with a distinctive, slightly squeaky timbre sometimes described as metallic. Voicing varies from softer, conversational 'jip's from birds in a feeding flock to the louder, more explosive flight call of a bird flying over woodland in the example (cf. song at 62 for various softer voicings).

Linnet calls are clipped, percussive notes delivered in rhythmic runs, broadly similar to Greenfinch. In contrast Linnet calls generally have a richer, percussive timbre and are delivered in characteristic fast, stuttering, though tuneful motifs. Nevertheless they vary like the other finch contact calls and can suggest other species on occasions. The calls in the first example are from birds in a pre-breeding flock, with some song snatches in the background.

Twite contact calls are very similar to Linnet, but the notes have a softer attack, with a more Brambling-like wheezy twang, though higher-pitched than the latter. Note the nasal 'tchway' or 'tchooik' (Macmillan) calls at the beginning of the first example; similar, though distinct calls are given by Brambling, Linnet and Goldfinch. The bird takes flight at the end of the last example.

Goldfinches usually call with rippling, liquid phrases of 'wit'- or 'tip'-type notes - 'stikelitt' (LJ); generally very distinctive, sometimes calls in flight can, on occasion, sound more like Linnet or Greenfinch. Birds in pre-breeding parties in the spring weave more elaborate calling motifs as they begin to sing (the bird in the second example, with others in the background).

Siskins have a rather complex vocabulary of calls, several of which are frequently given in flight, possibly depending on the season and the nature of the party or flock. The three main types are based on a fairly clear-toned, slightly disyllabic and descending 'teu' (as in the first example and cf. also 87), a more wheezy 'tewlee' or 'cheelu' (as in the second example and in 87) and chattering 'chit's, with a Linnet-like timbre, but often in more Greenfinch-like runs.

In flight, **Redpolls** tend to give one or both of two calls: a rattling trill call, also used for song in display flights in the breeding season, and more typically finch-like, rhythmic repetitions of notes with quite an abrasive sound - 'chichichi' in the examples. The guides refer to another call for Redpoll, a nasal 'tchewick' (Macmillan), a rising 'dyuee' (LJ) and a plaintive 'dsooee' (BWP); this is quite variable and potentially similar to the equivalent calls of several other finch species, so is less distinctive if unfamiliar. The flight call of Arctic Redpoll is said to be slower (LJ) (cf. also Redpoll calls during the Brambling song at 50).

More contact & alarm calls   94

Snow Bunting, Lapland Bunting, Yellowhammer, Shore Lark, Rock Pipit, Meadow Pipit

Snow Bunting and Lapland Bunting have similar sets of calls, the most frequent calls of each species being a little rippling or 'tickety' trill (the usual flight call) and monosyllabic notes variable from typically-bunting brief thin 'chit's to richer, Bullfinch-like 'teu's.

   Listen for the softer, bubbling quality in the **Snow Bunting** trills and apart from the distinctly flutey, descending 'teu' (0'14"), the other softer 'chee' ('pee' - BWP) and raspy 'chuh' (LJ) calls tend to hold their pitch. In contrast the **Lapland Bunting** trilled calls have a slightly harder, dry, tickety sound ('ti-li-li-lit' Macmillan, 'prrrrt' LJ); the 'teu' calls have a slightly wheezy or nasal timbre and the down-slurred pitch gives them a plaintive impression. Listen also to song at 64 for other examples of calls and see the text there for calls on breeding territories. **Yellowhammer** 'trlp'-type contact and alarm

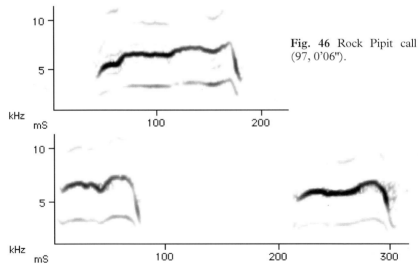

Fig. 46 Rock Pipit call (97, 0'06").

Fig. 47 Meadow Pipit calls (97, 0'23").

calls, often brief and almost disyllabic, are usually more extended trills in flight similar to Snow Bunting (listen to the last call in the example).

Shorelark calls are characterised by a pure-toned, bell-like, 'i' sound, pronounced 'ee' in English (BWP). The calls in the example are in loose 2 or 3 syllabled motifs, like 'tseet-eet', and are reported as the usual flight call.

Experienced birders maintain it is possible to distinguish between the flight calls of **Rock Pipit** and **Meadow Pipit** by ear, both a kind of 'tseep' or 'peest' (LJ), more metallic in the former species and less hissing the latter (BWP); two examples of each are given and the differences can be heard to be very slight. The Meadow Pipit calls are clipped, rather sharp notes, making the voice sound thinner and weaker (Macmillan) in contrast to the fuller impression of Rock's more sustained notes.

Wagtail calls 98

Yellow Wagtail, Grey Wagtail, Pied Wagtail, Swallow

Yellow Wagtail contact-alarm calls are generally single syllables - a rising 'tsweep' (possibly more associated with flight) and even-pitched or down-slurred 'tseee's, which seem interchangeable. In the British race (*flavissima*) it is said calls may be prolonged and disyllabic (BWP); the calls in the second example may be something like what is meant. The calls of *flava* are reported as sharper and those of *iberiae* and *feldegg* harsher than *flava*. In contrast the usual flight call of **Grey Wagtail** is a double note, with the rapid repetition of a single explosive syllable, giving a sibilant chinking sound. The first example is of a bird in flight, the second from a more alarmed, perched bird. The usual flight call of **Pied Wagtail**, the famous 'chissik' or such-like, has a marked disyllabic form, but a similar shrill sibilance to Grey Wagtail. White Wagtail, *alba* race, is said usually to give a more monosyllabic 'psit'-type call (BWP). Several birds call in the example; note the even pitch and emphasis of the two syllables compared to the **Swallow**'s alarm calls following, in which the accent falls on the second, lower-pitched syllable.

REFERENCES & FURTHER READING

BWP

S.Cramp (ed) (1977) *The Handbook of the Birds of Europe, the Middle East and North Africa: the Birds of the Western Palaearctic.* OUP.

Macmillan

A.Harris, L.Tucker & K.Vinicombe (1989) *The Macmillan Field Guide to Bird Identification.* Macmillan.

LJ

L.Jonsson (1992) *Birds of Europe (with North Africa and the Middle East).* Christopher Helm.

HFP

H.Heinzel, R.Fitter & J.Parslow (1995) *Collins Pocket Guide to Birds of Britain & Europe.* HarperCollins.

PMH

R.Peterson, G.Mountfort & P.Hollom (1965) *Collins Field Guide to the Birds of Britain and Europe.* HarperCollins

Catchpole & Slater

C.K.Catchpole & P.J.B.Slater (1995) *Bird Song - Biological themes and variations.* CUP.

Thorpe

W.H.Thorpe (1961) *Experimental Biology 12 - Bird-Song.* CUP.

Simms

E.Simms (1985) *New Naturalist: British Warblers.* HarperCollins.

Burton & Johnson

J.F.Burton & E.D.H.Johnson (1984) Insect, amphibian or bird? *British Birds* 77 (3) pp. 87-104.

JCR

J.C.Roché (1993) *All the bird songs of Britain & Europe* (on 4 CDs). Sittelle (Now called Bird Songs and Calls of Britain and Europe).

NSA

R.Kettle & R.Ranft of the National Sound Archive (eds) (1992) *British Bird Sounds on CD.* The British Library.

TYBS

D.Couzens & J.Wyatt (1992) *Teach Yourself Bird Sounds.* Waxwing Associates (Series of cassettes).

Bird Songs & Calls

G.Sample (1996) *The Collins Field Guide to Bird Songs & Calls.* HarperCollins.

R.Jellis (1977) *Bird Sounds and their Meaning.* BBC.

R.A.Hinde (ed) (1969) *Bird Vocalizations. Their relation to current problems in biology and psychology.* CUP.

E.A.Armstrong (1963) *A Study of Bird Song.* OUP.